Self-Transformation Through Music

Cover art by *Jane A. Evans*

Self-Transformation Through Music

Joanne Crandall

This publication made possible with the assistance of the Kern Foundation

The Theosophical Publishing House
Wheaton, Ill. U.S.A.
Madras, India/London, England

A publication of the Theosophical Publishing House, a department of the Theosophical Society in America.

Library of Congress Cataloging in Publication Data

Crandall, Joanne
  Self-transformation through music.
  (A Quest book)
  "This publication made possible with the assistance of the Kern Foundation."
  "A Quest original"—T.p. verso.
  1. Music therapy. I. Title.
ML3920.C887 1986   615.8'5154   86-40127
ISBN 0-8356-0608-2 (pbk.)

Printed in the United States of America

Dedicated to the first musician in my life—Ruth Colt, my mother

Contents

Acknowledgments

I wish to thank my children: Lisa Allan, Cathy Milligan, Debra, Michael, Melanie, and Larry Crandall, for the friendship and teachings and love they give to me.

For their continued encouragement, support, and helpful suggestions concerning this book, as well as for their goodness to me, I warmly thank Sanderson Beck, Lynn Frances, Jerry and Phyllis Glanville, Carolyn Kenny, Shirley Kalberg Leak, Teresa Milligan, and Brock Travis.

I particularly wish to acknowledge the work of Shirley Nicholson, Senior Editor at Quest, whose clarity and insight have contributed greatly.

Introduction

This is a book about music. It is also about relationship, connection, wholeness. I have written it as an
expression of gratitude for my experiences resulting
from the application of inner, spiritual truths to my
work in the field of music.

As a professional jazz pianist who has been working
in restaurants and nightclubs most of my adult life,
I was rapidly approaching burnout a couple of years
ago. I decided I wanted to stop performing and
become a music therapist instead. As a preparation
for this transition, I began using the restaurant in
which I play as a training ground for my work as
therapist. Through this process I learned an important
truth: that healing may take place anywhere, with
anyone, through the conscious, loving use of music. I
began applying inner spiritual techniques I had
learned to my audiences, using music as the instrument of healing. The result has been a complete
reversal in my attitudes about my work, my listeners,
my music, and myself. The changes have been
rapid and dramatic. Perhaps this book may serve as a
guide not only for other performing musicians who
feel the need to make changes in their attitudes

about their work, but for anyone wanting to experience the inner, spiritual qualities of music more fully.

Reading a book about music is a little like perusing a menu in a restaurant: the words, the descriptions, the ideas are at best symbols far removed from the reality of sound or of taste. No one has been able to discover the essence of a peach by reading about it, hearing it described, seeing a photograph of it, or by looking at the peach itself. Only by biting into it, tasting, chewing, swallowing, digesting, truly becoming one with it, can the essence of a peach be known.

So it is with music. The descriptions of a piece of music by a critic are meaningless to me. I can only know the music by experiencing it through all of my physical, intellectual, and emotional faculties working together to make the music a part of myself. By hearing, feeling, acknowledging the sound with all aspects of my being, the essence of the music is made available to my inner spirit. Reading about music cannot make this happen.

This book, then, is partly theory—ideas and thoughts about music—and it is partly suggestions on ways to test those ideas through actual personal experience. For me these two together make the only valid mode of learning. Reading the book through may provide some insight into the nature of music, of the musician, of the listener, and of the relationship existing between them. But without participating in the exercises, the concepts will remain intellectual ideas disconnected from your own reality. The exercises are designed to facilitate experiences that may bring you to a real knowing, a holistic understanding of the ideas set forth.

The exercises are simple, usually brief, requiring a little concentration and a lot of relaxation. They also seem to require a certain amount of trust: faith in the exercises, certainly, but more importantly, trust in your own ability to experience music in new and what may seem to be unorthodox ways. This means trust in the inner Knower or spirit, the part of you that may not often be consciously acknowledged or nurtured. The exercises can be viewed as a gift to spirit, a flexing of the soul muscles, just as physical exercise works the muscles of the material body and intellectual study stimulates and feeds the mind. The heart, too, will be moved and opened and expanded as you perform the exercises. When this happens, the windows and doors to the inner Self spring open, ready for nourishment and the consequential pouring forth of that spiritual energy that enriches and enhances our lives.

It is preferable to do the exercises as soon as possible after reading the preceding material. This will bring about an experiential reality that includes your mental, physical, and emotional states of being. Find a quiet place and a period of time when you are unlikely to be interrupted. Wear nonrestrictive clothing and no shoes. Most of the exercises may be done alone; a few are designed for partners or a group. A tape recorder with cassette is an invaluable aid and is essential for some of the exercises. Not only will it record what is happening, it will also give you images and visions of yourself and of your music that may be entirely new to you. Prepare for each exercise with a few deep, slow breaths; a brief prayer or summons of the spirit may seem appropriate. The more open and reverent your attitude toward the exercises, the more you will gain from them, as you keep in mind that you are the giver as well as the receiver.

Do not expect particular, prechosen results from your experiments. Things will be happening on levels that do not follow our usual expectations of effort and result, method and goal. Everything is happening at once, so to speak; part of the practice is to let go of linear time.

Helpful attitudes for doing the exercises may include attention, suspension of judgment, stillness, reverence, relaxation, lightness. They are not difficult; they are fun. They are also serious and deep. Honor that depth and enjoy your experiences.

I

The Sound

Vibration

In the beginning was the Word, the sound of the mighty Aum, the first vibration: creator and sustainer of the universe. As the sound goes on, the world of matter and space and time continue to exist. We are living in this sea of sound. Physicists are discovering the foundation of the universe to be not just matter, particles, atoms or quarks, but also movements of energy, vibration. This view of reality, seen for centuries by poets and mystics, is now beginning to be shared by some so-called materialists, the scientists.

It is as difficult or impossible to imagine a beginning of the universe as it is to envision its finish, its demise. It may be easier to view our world as a series of vibrations, certain frequencies originating in a range of sound that always exists—changing form, creating, destroying, evolving. In this view there is no start or finish but rather a continuous flow of energy.

As we begin to acknowledge the existence of this primal sound, this vibratory reality of the universe, we may gain an overall perspective encompassing its spiritual as well as its physical nature. This broader view is necessary if we wish to tune into the oneness of life and to recognize our own inherent unity with that one life.

When we use our physical senses exclusively as modes of perception, we are unable to hear the sound of the whole. Our ears pick up the grosser vibrations, our eyes discern the less subtle colors of the spectrum. We cannot know the origin, the cause of our existence without the use of the nonphysical aspect of our being—the intuition and the spirit. This involves letting go of the rational mind to journey within the realms of our own psyche wherein the universe is reflected.

The first step, then, in the recognition of the primal cosmic vibration is to move willingly within ourselves. As we make this journey, we will find the outer world revealed to us in direct proportion to the extent of the discoveries of our own inner being. For many, the preparation for this conscious journey may require a lifetime or many lifetimes. Often pain and suffering motivate us to move inward. Some of the more fortunate souls seem to be born with the desire to find the Self, or God, and spend their entire lives in conscious pursuit of that goal.

By virtue of music, the musician is consciously or unconsciously tuned into the vibrations of the cosmos, because music is the earthly, material mode for revealing the harmony of the universe to the physical ear. To become aware of the extent of that attunement, to move more deeply into oneself, and at the same time to open with more awareness to the vibrations that surround us—this will bring us into full musicianship. Such an awareness brings out our creativity and acknowledges our connection to and oneness with the whole.

The starting point for some musicians on this journey of consciousness may be signalled by a decreasing joy in the experience of composing or performing. Of all earthly occupations, music may have the closest relationship to reality and therefore to joy. When joy in music diminishes or disappears it is time to move within to discover the origin of our being in vibration, sound, music. Without connection to that source, our music loses life and beauty and even meaning.

Increasing joy is available to musicians and all those who include music as an integral part of their lives. If we can open to our own beingness and make the Self available to others through music, at higher levels we are resonating with the Word, the Aum, the creative, vibratory force and sustainer of the cosmos. We have the opportunity to embark upon this odyssey openheartedly, mindfully (but not necessarily intellectually), and with faith that we are discovering our true selves as human beings, as lovers of music and musicians, not only at the end of the journey, but all along the way as well.

We exist in an ocean of sound. We create music when we bring the vibratory waves into a hearable, observable, material form. Musicians drop their net into the sea and bring up those parts of themselves with which they are consciously or unconsciously in touch. The dreamer creates the dream and molds the material into a form he or she can accept and honor, then pours it forth into the world as music.

As musicians become aware of and tune into higher and finer vibrations, music becomes a powerful tool for the evolution and transformation of our individual consciousness and for the transformation of the consciousness of the planet.

Rhythm: Pulse

Our bodies are rhythm instruments. At the very start of life there is the heartbeat of the embryo, identical with that of the mother, later becoming a separate pulse. The womb resonates with the sound of the pulse of life. At birth, the infant begins breathing, a rhythmic cycle of in, out, inhale, exhale that will continue in tandem with the heartbeat until the moment of death. Throughout our journey in this physical body, the pulse of life continues, racing in excitement, slowing while sleeping, becoming erratic at times of emotional or physical stress. The body's rhythm parallels and reflects and is one with the pulse of the universe. The dance goes on, and we are dancing all our lives.

Music connects us in direct and discernible ways with our own rhythmical instrument, the body, and also with the outer world. Whether we hear the lilting, three-quarter beat of a Strauss waltz, the seventeen-beat cycle of an Indian raga, or the uncountable, subtle underlying rhythm of an avant garde composition, the body recognizes and responds to the pulse of the music. We are compelled to tap our feet, slow our breath, join in the dance the music is describing.

Musicians are always aware of the body's rhythm as it corresponds to the beat of the music. They seem to have been born with this rhythmic consciousness; the difference between musicians and so-called nonmusicians may be that the former have never forgotten their connection with the pulse of life. They feel it in every cell of their bodies as the pulse carries oxygen and nourishment through the arteries; they express the throbbing flow in their movements, in their voices, through their instruments. It is virtually impossible for them to lose contact with this rhythm. To be "out of synch" with it is a symptom of disharmony, dis-ease.

Rhythm involves repetition: it is the base, the ground from which all else emerges. As the heartbeat is the ground of our physical being, so the pulse of the universe is inherent in all of life.

Exercise: Rhythm, Pulse

1. Sit quietly in a relaxed, comfortable position, breathing gently. Place your fingers on your pulse at the neck or the wrist until you become familiar with the feel of your own heartbeat.

After a few moments of quiet attention, begin moving softly, gently, nodding your head, rocking from side to side, any movement that seems simple and appropriate. Use your heartbeat as the underlying rhythm for the movement. Observe without judgment the flow of your body as it is orchestrated by your heartbeat. You might imagine your heartbeat emerging from the floor, providing a ground, a base, for your movement.

2. Turn your tape player on record. After a few

moments of quiet attention, begin playing or singing, using your heartbeat as the underlying rhythm for the music. Continue playing until you feel the inner signal to stop.

Now play back what has been recorded. You may wish to move or dance to the music, feeling the connection between your heartbeat and your body through the channel of your own music. Again, observe without judgment the flow of your movements that have been orchestrated by your music. You might imagine your heartbeat emerging from the floor, providing a ground, a base, for the music and your movements.

3. During the day, in the midst of your activities—walking, talking, listening to or playing music—pause for a moment. Place your fingers on your pulse. Feel your heartbeat describing the rhythm of your body, connecting you to the rhythm of life around you.

Energy: Breath

Our life as a physical being depends upon breath, the taking in and breathing out of air. In the womb the mother's breath carries nourishment to the unborn child. At the moment of birth, the infant begins breathing on its own. In astrological terms, that first breath determines the circumstances of the child's birth: the position of the stars and planets in space which affect the vibratory waves of consciousness present at the moment when time and space come into being for the newly-born. All the contents of the material world interpenetrate the child with its first breath. That breath continues in synergistic union with the heartbeat throughout life.

The breath carries the same energy that permeates the universe. In different cultures it is variously called shakti, prana, chi'i, or simply life force. Perhaps the best, most inclusive and descriptive definition is that which unifies us all through breath.

Every breath we take draws into our bodies the same energy that is shared by every living being on the planet. I cannot separate "my" air from that of my neighbor. I cannot isolate, save, or horde the air I exhale from the rest of the world. The inevitability of the oneness of breath, of the common denominator of the air we breathe, is becoming increasingly evident as the conflict between smokers and non-smokers intensifies. We are reaching an awareness that that which we breathe in and out of our bodies is the common property of all.

The lark takes in breath, then exhales it as lilting melody. The breeze, invisible and immeasurable, rustles the leaves of the aspen and music is created. Musicians recognize and honor the breath as the stream upon which tone, pitch, volume, emotion, and beauty depend. They consciously utilize this common stream. The flutist breathes life energy through a hollow tube to produce sound. The singer uses the instrument of the body to transform energy into song. Even when the breath is not directly involved with the production of tone, as in playing a percussion or stringed instrument, for example, still it plays an essential role in the creation of music.

All performers experience the acceleration of the breath that occurs with the onset of stage fright. Many musicians practice some sort of breath awareness such as meditation or yoga to bring the technique of conscious, gentle breathing into their playing. They realize that the breath enhances their creativity and their artistic ability.

Through being aware of the breath and feeling the flow of life energy or prana moving through the body, musicians bring to their music and to their listeners the awareness of the one force that moves, sustains, and permeates the universe. The musician is the reminder of our oneness in the breath we all share.

Exercise: Breath, Energy

1. Sit comfortably, eyes closed. If you play an instrument, keep it close at hand. Become aware of your breath as it flows in and out. Feel the movement of your chest and diaphragm. Observe the sensation in your nostrils as the air moves through them.

Allow the breath to deepen and gradually slow down. Feel the pause, the hesitation occurring between one breath and the next. Imagine that the breath is carrying the unifying universal energy into your body, journeying through the bloodstream, nourishing all the organs, every cell.

Then as you exhale, contribute your own life energy, your unique, personal love, to the universal energy as it pours out, enhancing and enriching the world supply in the same way you are enriched by the energy coming in on your breath.

You may feel a sound moving on the flow of breath. Let that sound—a sigh, a moan, a whisper—come forth. Feel the inhaled breath flowing out in a sound of love. Hear the sound as a tangible manifestation of prana, the energy of the universe.

2. When you feel ready, begin singing or playing your instrument. If you are singing or playing a wind instrument, feel the inhaled breath flowing out again in tones of pure love. If you are playing a different kind of instrument, feel the breath-energy flowing into that instrument. Hear the emerging music as a tangible manifestation of prana, the energy of the universe.

Time: Cycles

Time is of the essence, or so it seems on this physical plane of existence. We measure our lives linearly, chronologically, in decades, years, days, minutes. We work and eat and sleep by a system loosely paralleling the daily cycle of the revolutions of the planet. We pattern our years by the somewhat drastic physiological, emotional, and psychological changes marking the onset of cycles of being: childhood, puberty, adulthood, middle and old age. To the extent that we recognize and flow with these cycles, our lives proceed organically and naturally. There are seasons of growth and development; there are corresponding periods of rest and dormancy. The woman's most obvious cycle is the menses, the onset of which marks the beginning of puberty and which continues to the end of her childbearing years. This exclusively female cycle that coincides with the cycles of the moon and tides may bring woman into far closer contact with nature, with Mother Earth, than man, lacking such a clearly visible cycle, can hope to attain.

Music connects us with the cyclic nature of life. In Western traditional music, the notes are measured mathematically, precisely, into bars, phrases, movements, based generally on cycles of two, four, eight, sixteen. Eastern music is freer but is still bound by time cycles. In the new music which has been emerging since the late nineteenth and early twentieth centuries, precise cycles have become less evident. It is interesting that as science devises ways of splitting time into ever smaller parts, to the millionth of a second, and as people wear watches recording the time to the hundredth of a second, music is less concerned with the whole concept of linear time. It is becoming more and more cyclical. Minimalist composers, such as Terry Riley and Steve Reich, build sound upon layers of repetitive, rhthmic motifs which continue with little alteration throughout an entire piece. Indian music and the gamelan music of Indonesia are precursors of this cyclic style of composition. In some avant garde scores, notes are placed on a circular staff rather than in straight lines; the individual musicians are invited to join or quit the circle of sound as they see fit. The new music is very much in touch with the reality of cycles, of the circle, even of the sphere, such as the Earth.

Mystics describe the contents of eternity as all that exists in the present moment. Their formula for inner peace, for the discovery of heaven on earth, is to live in the Now, the eternal present, free of yesterday's regret and tomorrow's fear. Music can bring us to the awareness of the eternal Now because it can be experienced only in the present. As we engage our full attention in the music, we are in the present moment. A pitfall of participating exclusively in familiar forms of music is that expectation creeps in: we are not totally engaged in sound as it

17

is happening but instead eagerly await what we know will follow. Eastern Indian music and Western jazz minimize this expectation through their highly improvisational nature. We may perhaps gauge our ability to be in the present moment by our willingness to listen to and participate in unfamiliar or improvisational music.

Each moment in time is the only moment there is. This moment is not measured linearly. The sound emerging from this moment is the only sound. It is free of the past or the future. The sound may be a single note or a phrase or an entire piece of music, existing as the eternal moment, the Now, free of linear considerations of time—bound up with infinity.

Exercise: Time, Cycles

Breathing softly and gently, allow a sound or a tone to come forth. Or if an instrument is available, play a single note. Listen to the sound of your voice or the instrument; follow it until it has completely faded away. Place your full, loving attention upon the sound, knowing that as long as the sound continues you are in the present moment. This has nothing to do with seconds or minutes.

Now experiment with a sequence of sounds, a phrase, part of a melody. Feel your body interpenetrated, permeated, immersed in the phrase. Do not attempt to define or judge in any way; simply feel yourself within the sound. Hear nothing but the sound. The duration of the phrase becomes the Now.

Play or listen to an entire piece of music in this way, hearing nothing but the sound in an eternal moment when time stands still.

Melody and Tone

Melody is the most readily accessible aspect of music. We hum, sing, or play a string of notes, and something melodic occurs. A simple melody can produce immediate pleasure. Spoken words gain tremendous power when joined with melody to create a song. Native Americans used this power of song for virtually all their activities: hunting, planting crops, healing.

We seem to respond to melody for its simplicity and, because it signifies one of our greatest needs as humans, that of relationship. A melody is a series of tones existing in relationship with each other to form a whole—a relationship of interval or space, of time, of pitch, and of volume. A single tone by itself is not a melody. Only as it exists with other tones different from itself does a melody emerge.

The musician with a trained ear (trained, that is, in the Western sense) can identify the differences in tones that constitute a particular melody, but this ability does not necessarily enhance listening pleasure. It may even be a hindrance because the identifying, classifying mind also judges, thereby closing the door to heartfelt appreciation of the music.

There can be no objective standards for the worth of a melody. We bring to our listening our own experience and our individual mode of being, which influences our way of hearing. There may be some sort of general enjoyment in listening to a so-called "soaring" melody, but there is no perfect series of tones forming a melody everyone can love. The reaction of liking or disliking, determining good or bad, seems to stem from the underlying harmony or rhythm of a piece rather than from the melody itself, which in its simplicity appeals to something other than the mind. The melody gives the mind a rest; it provides space for the heart to open and receive the music.

The single tone incorporated into the relationship called a melody may symbolize us individually as we relate to others. Space, time, and experience all play a role in determining the quality of the emerging melody, the relationship between each of us and the rest of the world. The melody and the music constantly change as we move and grow, as space and time and experience flow around us and through us. At times the melody may seem to cease for a while as we withdraw from others and move within. We may remain apart from the melody, sounding our individual tone, unwilling or unable to bond with others. There can be no meaning in life without deep relationship, just as there can be no song without melody.

Our conscious and willing interaction with each other creates an element of beauty in our lives and brings meaning to our existence. A simple melody can remind us of our interrelationship, our undeniable connection with each other and with all of life. Whether or not we choose to join our tone with that of others and participate in the flow of the melody, we are all part of the one song.

Exercise: Melody and Tone

Hum or play a line of a familiar melody, feeling its wholeness and beauty. Repeat it, omitting one specific tone each time it occurs in the melody. Observe what happens to the continuity, the flow, the sound of the melody when that note is missing.

Rudolf Steiner, German occultist and founder of the Anthroposophical Society, saw esoteric and meaningful relationships between the intervals of the Western musical scale. Here are some ways you may discover your own meanings in these intervals:

1. If you have an instrument, play middle C, then the fifth above, G. (If you don't have an instrument, go on to exercise 2.) Feel the "space" between the tones. In the West we arbitrarily call this a fifth but in the Eastern mode of quarter tones it may be something else. Listen without naming. Play other intervals. Compare the feelings evoked from hearing a third, a sixth, a seventh, an octave, always remaining aware of the relationship existing between notes, defining the intervals through sound rather than intellectually.

2. Stand comfortably with eyes closed. Allow a tone to arise gently from your heart area and hum it. Feel it resonating in your chest, your head, throughout your body. Now hum a second tone, different from the first. Allow your body to move in such a way as to express the aural space between the two tones. Observe your body movements as you flow from one tone to the other and back again.

Now hum a simple melody quite slowly. Let your body represent the melody. Feel the intervals, the space, the movement of tones as corresponding movements of your arms, legs, head, torso. Let your body be the melody.

Silence

Silence is not the absence of sound. So long as the world exists as a physical, material entity, vibration or sound is present. Silence is the womb in which sound is conceived and nourished, the matrix from which it emerges into the world of time and space and audibility. Silence is dynamic: from silence was born the Word, Creator of life and worlds and beings. In the womb, sound is germinating and growing, as well as being formed by the silence in which it is sheltered. As the womb of the mother stretches and alters to accommodate the developing fetus, so the silence expands and changes, allowing the development of the soon-to-be-born sound.

As we sit in meditation, we may become so still that the vibrations and sounds of silence become audible: the rushing of blood through the arteries; the whooshing of air in and out the nostrils; the drumming of the heartbeat. Beyond these, we may even hear whistling, bells, ringing—sounds of the eternal Silence within.

The tension, the movement, the energy of silence—this is the other side of music. The musician is informed by the silence of what is to be born. And as the music ends and sound subsides into vibrations moving beyond the range of the human ear, new sounds are already coming into being in the silence. The musician pours these forth as new tones, new music.

Silence does not occur exclusively between the tones of the music or during rhythmic pauses or at the end of a phrase. Silence is the ever-present ground from which sound arises. If this ground was removed, there could be no sound. This seems paradoxical: how can there be silence while sound is happening? The answer seems to lie in the reality that silence and sound are one—holographic, interdependent, and inclusive within each other. This interrelationship of sound and silence may be represented by the ancient Chinese symbols of yin and yang in the circle or sphere: the white dot of yang, sound, within the black yin, or silence; and the block dot of yin, silence, present in the white, yang, sound. This is not a static, unmoving unit but rather a flowing dynamic process.

It is an illuminating experience to hear music with a conscious awareness of the continual presence of silence within the sound. Tuning one's ears and being to the underlying, inherent silence of the music creates a feeling of wholeness, of completion. This experience is available to us in all sound but it is particularly evident in fine music of any idiom. Jazz musicians have an instinctive knowledge and understanding of the role of silence. Great jazz artists bring the consciousness of silence into their music in such a way that even the unaware listener is made to respond to it without knowing why the listening experience seems so magical.

Musicians use silence as they use sound: as an

essential means to produce music that speaks of their inner being, of the being of the listener, and of the relationship between them. Listen to the silence. It speaks and sings through the sound, creating, shaping, transforming life and power and beauty into music.

Exercise: Silence

1. Sit quietly, eyes closed. Become aware of your breathing; allow your attention to remain with the breath until you have contacted the stillness at your center. Sit in that stillness for a few moments. Thoughts may arise; allow them to pass, like clouds in the sky. Remain in touch with the stillness, the silence.

When you feel ready, allow the sounds within you to emerge from the silence. Feel that silence underlying the sound of your voice. Observe without judgment the qualities the silence seems to impart to the audible voice.

As the sound ends, let it move back into the center of silence within you. Feel how that center has been permeated and enriched by your sound.

2. If you have an instrument, start as above, watching your breathing until you can remain in touch with the stillness, the silence. Now begin playing your instrument. Feel the music emerging from your inner silence. Feel that silence all through the playing of the music. Observe without judgment the qualities the silence seems to impart to the audible sound.

As the music ends, let it move back into the center of silence within you. Feel how that center has been permeated and enriched by the music.

3. Sitting by the ocean, imagine the bottom of the sea. Be aware of the stillness, the quiet peacefulness under the surface of the water. Connect that stillness with your own inner silence. Begin moving, using your arms and legs like waves moving out from the center, the depth of the ocean within you.

4. Periodically observe a time of silence each day. Also try to set aside one whole day a week with no inner or outer talking.

Structure and Form

Our universe is an orderly one. Planets orbit the sun; the solar system progresses systematically through the galaxy; electrons whirl around their own suns, the protons and neutrons which comprise the nucleus of the atom. The seeds of birch trees eventually become birch trees; the infant matures into adulthood, genetically similar to its parents. The days and nights, the seasons, the tides move in a consistent, reliable flow. For the human being, alone and afraid, an orderly universe is reassuring. It spells protection, safety. The ground of our being is the Earth, traveling predictably in its course around our source of life, the sun. Without this certainty, life would be unbearable.

Music is the reflection and the expression of that order. As our world was created through sound, so it becomes comprehensible to us through music. The dance of the waves and particles, the vibrations of the electromagnetic field, the movement of light—all are represented as sound in its most ordered form, music. As we experience music, we feel our connection with a world of design and order.

Difficulty arises, however, when we confuse order

with structure and form. Order persists throughout the whole evolution of a form: its conception, its realization, its eventual decay and dissolution. There can be no form without this underlying order. But whether there is a structure or not, and regardless of what form that structure may take, there is always order.

The end of structure or form is not the end of order.

This is important to remember when considering the arts, particularly music, the most fluid and least frozen of the arts. We tend to place our faith in the existing structures of our own culture, our own personal forms, the ones with which we are most familiar. This is a valid faith. But clinging doggedly to these forms when they no longer reflect the evolutionary reality can freeze us in an unreal, illusionary moment of the past.

Music not only reflects the evolution of life; it is one with the process of growth and change. Composers are not just prophets; they are orchestrators of the flow of life in the present moment. They have the willingness and the ability to hold past traditions with a light, open hand, using them as needed but allowing them to slip away as the world and music and consciousness change and evolve. For the listener, a corresponding surrender of the past is needed to be truly in tune with life's flow.

Our ears are conditioned by our culture, by our personal likes and dislikes, based on our experience and our view of the world. It is perfectly valid to honor these perspectives. In using music as therapy for elderly persons, the most direct path to their hearts is often through the particular musical idioms with which they identify: classical, gay nineties, country western, religious, folk, or ethnic music. We may journey all through life never having our musical preferences challenged, except perhaps by exposure to the current "pop" style such as: rock, funk, punk. We may never venture into a concert offering the new music of Boulez or Cage. We may never hear the music of the gamelan orchestra of Indonesia, the koto of Japan, the sitar of India.

We live in a global village in which communication and understanding of one another are now essential for the preservation of the planet. Do we have time to learn the spoken languages, the customs, the philosophies of our neighbors? The most immediate and effective method of communication with our global friends may be in listening to, becoming familiar with, or performing the music of other peoples. The music of a culture describes its people, their roots, their desires and highest strivings. To be able to listen to their music with unconditioned ears is a remarkable means of moving closer to the people. A way to the heart is through music; the broader the musical preferences, the wider that path becomes.

Open ears are willing to surrender old concepts of what is structurally correct or beautiful or uplifting. To allow structure its demise, to hear music as formless, orderly but without boundaries—this is a necessary step in the coming together of parent and child, American and Russian, Muslim and Jew, self and Self. We live in a world of no boundaries. Music reflects that world most accurately when it is allowed to flow and evolve as life itself evolves. There is no music without movement; motion is inherent in the music itself and in its reflection of culture and consciousness.

Our ears are capable of hearing a great deal more than we choose to listen to. Clinging to tried and true forms may be like continuing to wear the clothes of childhood. Outgrown, ragged, outdated, they are no longer of any use to us. We may need new clothes, perhaps at times no clothes. At the very least, we might examine our need for the old clothes, the old forms. What are we holding onto? Why can we not let go? Perhaps our willingness to broaden our musical horizons may be linked to our ability to open to life, to flow with it in acceptance and enthusiasm.

To see structure and form as fluid, soft, flexible, always flowing and changing may be the ideal in appreciating, composing, or performing music. Even music of the past changes and evolves as it is played by new musicians and heard by new listeners. Mozart's music has been with us for centuries, existing in a sort of field that is moved, acted upon, refined, defined anew by every musician who has ever performed his works. A new music emerges, still Mozart's structures and forms but fluid and evolving—timeless.

Structure may remain fairly stable, as Mozart's has, or it may alter or disappear, as in the new music of the avant garde. To feel structure as part of the flow, as one with the evolution of life, brings new meaning to the word. It is no longer stiff, rigid, unmoving, frozen in the time from which it emerged. As we view structure from this perspective and discover order apart from, as well as within, form, we are free to surrender to the river of life reflected and created by music.

Exercise: Structure and Form

Choose a piece of music that is entirely new to you, something you have never heard. South Indian vocal music may be a challenging choice. For a week, listen to it once or twice a day, or more often if you have the time. As judgments of the mind or emotional reactions arise, allow them full rein without losing touch with the experience of listening.

As the piece becomes more familiar, observe your thoughts and feelings. Are they changing? Are there openings occurring at the mind and heart levels?

Purpose: Meaning

"What is the meaning of this?" We begin asking this question early in life; we go on asking as we grow and change and are moved by events and relationships, which are the content of our lives. We search for meaning and purpose in our work, within our families, in our outer and inner worlds. As we discover some sort of purpose or design for our existence, we feel fulfilled. When change or loss occurs, we are confused and fearful, until meaning begins to emerge. A reason for being, a meaning for existence, seems to be a necessity for everyone. This need may become most evident in our search for God.

We extend our need for meaning into our experience of music as composer, listener, or performer. Art provides meaning in various ways: it may depict the reality of the present; it may be historical or ethnic, connecting us with our roots, our heritage; it may concern itself with the future, prophesying what we may expect in our lives and in the world. Music, art, drama, dance, literature may be seen as mirrors of our reality, reflecting who and where we are, why we are, *that* we are. The arts are essential for our pursuit of meaning.

Western music is particularly involved in the role of art as a literal symbol of meaning. We hear symphonic works describing firework displays, wars, love trysts, death, rebirth, the entire gamut of human experience. We listen to pastoral works describing the beauties of nature; we hear great choral masses glorifying God; we enjoy tender, romantic pieces designed to open and move our hearts to love. These kinds of music can be uplifting, ennobling, beautiful. They serve us well in our search for meaning in the outer world.

When we hear a composition for the first time, however, unaware of the title or the composer's intentions, what meaning may be ascribed to the work? How clearly and freely can our own meaning emerge after we have been told what the music is about, what it is describing or attempting to evoke? Descriptive music that purports to be about something may serve a purpose. But sound, in and of itself, has no meaning; it is simply sound. It is descriptive or evocative of nothing more than what is present in the heart and mind of the listener. As human beings, we are vehicles of meaning: we project our own interpretations, our own thoughts and feelings, onto the outer world. We imbue our lives and art with purpose that originates within ourselves. When we can find no meaning in a work of art, we are really saying that that particular piece does not reflect a recognizable aspect of our own psyche. This may be a key to our attraction for certain music: it is providing an echo of the cry within the heart for illumination.

Our own symbols or meanings may emerge more clearly if we reject the preconditioning of titles, explorations of the composer's intentions, or declarations of musicologists and critics. When we are experiencing familiar music, this may prove to be difficult. Listening to Beethoven's Sixth Symphony is apt to turn our thoughts to a pasture full of cattle, a less than reassuring prospect for some. To stand at the base of the General Sherman tree in Sequoia National Park, for example, may encourage us to think of wars and separation and violence against our brothers. How much nicer to just be with the tree as it is—an ancient, living being with which we are intimately and irrevocably at one.

To go beyond description or definition and find our own personal meaning in the clear still waters of universality reflected by great art is the evolutionary step we are now approaching. The next step in human consciousness may be in moving beyond the need for meaning and purpose. The rational, logical, divisive mind seeks reasons and goals. To drop the need to understand the world and simply to *be* in the world, in life, in music—this may be the new direction of humanity. Relinquishing the desire for knowing may be necessary in our quest for self-knowledge. This kind of mindless, mindful, heartfelt beingness is nothing more than allowing the present moment to be the only moment. There is no meaning in the Now; there is only presence, consciousness, awareness of the richness, the holiness contained in this moment.

Composing, performing, or listening to music with our full attention upon the sound is to discover the life beyond description or meaning, the life that simply *is*. This is love work and heart work, not head work. It is not a process of doing but rather of letting go, allowing, watching, surrendering. It is a sort of death, a dying to each moment. Freed from the boundaries of mind, the heart opens to its connection, its oneness, with the energy of the universe that is inherent in sound and music. Perhaps true meaning may be found in that space of no meaning.

Exercise: Purpose, Meaning

Try this while listening to Vivaldi's "Four Seasons," which is a descriptive piece of music:

First listen while visualizing the seasons as the composer conceived and titled them. Move to the music; create dances of spring, summer, autumn, winter with your movements. Immerse yourself deeply in the images evoked by the music.

Now switch titles, so that Vivaldi's "Spring" becomes your winter, his "Autumn" your summer, and so on. Move to the music according to these different seasons. Observe any sense of freedom or of resistance that seems to occur.

Sit for a few moments in silence and draw from your being four entirely new titles for the four sections of Vivaldi's composition: for example river, ocean, mist, rain; or cats, dogs, snakes, pigs. Again listen and move to the music with these new titles. Observe without judgment the way your body moves; observe your physical and visual responses to the music.

Finally, sit quietly, eyes closed, listening to the music as pure sound: vibration, pitch, rhythm, melody, timbre. Allow the music to move through your body, unnamed, undefined. Feel the energy of the sound flowing through your cells. In silence and stillness, be filled with the music, become one with the sound.

35

Harmony and Dissonance

We are all seeking harmony in our lives—within ourselves, in our relationships with others, with the entirety of our existence. We tend to gravitate toward those with whom we are in accord, with whom we resonate; we try to avoid situations which threaten us with dissonance, separateness, dis-harmony. We view the natural world as harmonious and orderly, and we wish to bring our personal lives into affinity with that state.

Our concept of a harmonious universe is perfectly reflected in Western traditional music. Occultists such as Ouspensky and Rudolf Steiner found what they considered striking correlations between the octave with its intervals and the movement of the stars and planets. To our Western ears, the octave with its thirds and fifths seems to be the essence of harmony.

This view is being challenged by acquaintance with music of other traditions and even by the emerging music of our own contemporary culture. We are learning the deeper meanings of harmony as we are willing to admit dissonance as a necessary part of the whole. We may have to ask ourselves if there really is such a thing as dissonance when listening with an open, nonjudgmental mind.

Harmony has been described as the simultaneous happenings of pitches. While melody may be thought of as tones moving horizontally, so to speak, harmony is a sort of vertical stacking of tones. This harmony may be contrived according to our ideas of what is correct, appropriate, and pleasing. Or it may simply be what happens at a given moment, which may seem incorrect, inharmonious, and ugly. It is all harmony. There is no natural law based on acoustics or physics or the planets which determines harmony. Our minds, conditioned by our cultural and personal preferences, make that decision.

An octave played by itself sounds empty. It is not dissonant, but without other tones included within its boundaries, it is not harmonious either. It is like a picture frame with nothing inside. But is the world of sound no more than this? All sound, all tones, exist within the cosmos. If we listen to the flow of tones from one octave to the next, we hear that pure unconditioned sound unbroken by "intervals." This unbounded, uncircumscribed sound is always present. Are we willing to hear it?

Just as the universal sound, the Aum, is composed of all sound and is the fulfillment and embodiment of all the tones of the cosmos, and as all the vibrations of light are present in the white light, so we, too, are all sound and all colors. To recognize the Aum, we need to hear and accept all sounds within the One. To do this, we must let go our ideas of dissonance and harmony.

Is there anything resounding in the mighty Aum that could be called inharmonious? Are there any vibrations that are unnecesary or ugly or dissonant, except in our own minds? Vibration just *is*; definition or evaluation of one vibration, one sound, compared to another exists only in the finite mind.

In our striving for harmony, we cannot deny or ignore the sounds we would call dissonant. We cannot experience our wholeness by denying our "lower" parts: our negative emotions or thoughts, even our physical bodies. We are everything, all. To see ourselves as less, to exclude the seconds and fourths and sevenths, to separate ourselves into pleasing and unpleasing, positive and negative parts is to deny wholeness within ourselves and, concurrently, our oneness with all of life. To experience that oneness is to hear and accept the full spectrum of sound as harmonious and beautiful and to recognize our own corresponding spectrums of light and sound and being.

Exercise: Harmony and Dissonance

1. While walking along a noisy city street, stop, close your eyes, and with full attention listen to all the sounds around you. Immerse yourself in the cacophony of the traffic, the voices, all the jumbled noises of the city. Imagine the sounds as a great symphonic work not yet written by an unborn composer. Feel the noise as life, the whole of it, in that particular spot. Experience its energy, its diversity, its vitality, its Nowness, its crazy harmony.

Open your eyes and continue walking in the symphony. You may want to try this exercise in any noisy place: a children's crowded schoolroom, an aviary at the zoo, a factory.

2. With the sustain pedal on the piano depressed,

or on another instrument, play an A major chord. Listen to it until the sound with all its overtones has faded completely. Observe any thoughts or feelings that may arise as you are listening.

Now play the same chord, adding the seventh, G#. Without judgment, observe the responses of your body and your thoughts and feelings. Continue playing the chord, adding more and more of the notes contained within the octave, observing your responses to each new sound.

Finally, play a chord which includes every note within the octave. Feel that chord as an expression of the universe within and the universe without. Let the sound flow on until it has faded completely; feel yourself as that sound.

In the silence that follows, be aware of the continuation of vibration beyond the ear's ability to perceive. As you do this exercise, think in terms of complete or incomplete sound rather than of dissonance or resonance.

Finally, play an A major chord once more. How does it sound to you now?

Music and Feeling

We live in a world of movement, of feeling. As humans we are the vessels of all feeling: physical sensations such as temperature, pressure, touch; mind/ego attitudes such as anger, isolation, fear; and feelings of the heart like grief, love, sorrow, joy. Insofar as we acknowledge that we are creatures of feeling, and to the extent that we are in touch with our feelings, we are able to relate to ourselves and to the world in a valid way.

Feelings may be our most viable means of communication. Our ability to use language and speech may be at best a secondary tool. Animals communicate with each other nonverbally. Even plants communicate. For example, certain trees emit a chemical that not only repels potentially dangerous insects but triggers a similar reaction in neighboring trees as well.

Verbal language is invaluable, but it is limited. The mind and the ego are susceptible to misinterpretation of incoming information. Divorced from feeling, mind-talk is sterile, lifeless, ultimately without meaning. The language of the heart, the language of feeling, is the one in which we are able to reach others most completely and accurately.

To be in touch with and then express our feelings may be joyful, painful, scary, awful, or awesome. Regardless of our value judgments about our feelings, to feel and express them is life-affirming. It is our connection with our own humanness and with all of humanity. A friend of mine who is a political activist has this rule: he will not engage in an intellectual discussion with anyone until oneness has been experienced between them. This oneness occurs, he feels, not in the mind but in the heart.

Music has been a prime vehicle for the expression and communication of feeling throughout all of recorded history, and even in prehistoric times, the mythic ages. The mother's crooning lullaby to her infant; the drumming of the tribesman signaling to his people; the flutist breathing out expressions of longing and desire—music of the heart has been played since the beginning of time, moving us and expressing the heart of humanity. Passion, ecstasy, despair, wonder, love, pain; all the conditions of life are heard in and through music.

When we say we are "moved" by music, what is being moved? It is that innermost aspect of ourselves that resides in feeling. When we are grieving, a certain piece of music can move directly into that grief, deepening, defining, and expressing it in inexplicable ways. It brings us to an acknowledgment and acceptance of our grief. It prods the sorrow asking, "What is this grief? Where was it born? Feel its intensity; open to it, move with it, let it flow through you." Music provides a spaciousness for our feeling, room for it to breathe and expand.

We may be aware of the effects of certain music upon us, but its influence begins at deeply submerged areas of our psyche and acts on a level not engaged by the conscious mind. Thus music is a tremendous tool with unlimited possibilities for opening the contents of the unconscious, the hidden feelings, and raising them to a level of awareness where they may be observed, accepted, and eventually dealt with and expressed. Recently there has been increased interest in using music as therapy for emotionally disturbed people, not as a tranquilizer, but as a safe and effective means to explore the inner worlds.

Emotions are our feelings moving outwards. They are the outer expression of the contents of the heart. Music can be the mover of these feelings, the carrier, the stream on which our feelings flow outwards. Feelings that are stuck or blocked from our awareness can be awakened through music; our life is enhanced and enlivened by the richness of that inner world of feeling.

We may hear someone say, "Our children shouldn't be listening to acid rock. It's destructive; it promotes anger and violence." But it is important for that emerging anger to be acknowledged and observed. The anger resides in the self, not in the music. To uncover the anger, to observe it, to explore it, to become one with it is much more valuable then to let it fester at an unconscious level.

Music in itself is not manipulative, but some music has been blatantly designed to move and manipulate the emotions. When words or images are added, an effort has been made to shape or control feelings through the use of music. Most film scores and many pop and rock songs fall into this category. As we listen to music itself, without images or words superimposed upon it, our own feelings will arise naturally and spontaneously. The most effective type of music for the evocation rather than the manipulation of feeling may perhaps be the most subtle: a gentle Mozart sonatina or a simple melody played on un-accompanied violin.

Music affects everyone differently, in unprescribed and unpredictable ways, but it is intrinsically move-ment. As such, it has the power to reflect and touch and stir our inner movement, our inner world of feeling.

Exercise: Music and Feeling

Choose a recording of music that seems to move you deeply, for whatever reason. It may even be some-thing you dislike that makes you feel angry or confused: an Indonesian gamelan orchestra or acid rock, or Stravinsky.

Stand quietly, eyes closed. As the music begins, feel it moving like a river directly into your heart, as if through a door you have opened expressly for this purpose. Allow the music to move in your heart area, awakening, nudging, pushing and pulling at the feelings you have stored there.

As you become aware of the movement of these feelings, begin moving your body; allow your body to become the feelings. Through the motions of your arms, legs, head, torso, express the anger or joy or pain or sadness that has been stirred up in your heart. Let the music be your movement, your feelings; turn all responsibility for what you feel over to the music as you move. Feel the oneness of sound, body, feeling, movement, and the space in which it is all occurring.

As the recording ends, feel the music draw the movement and the feelings back into your heart area. Stand peacefully in the stillness and silence.

Music and Nature

The earth is our mother. We are composed of her elements, born of her soil. We walk upon her ground and breathe her air. From our first breath to our last, she nurtures and sustains us in this astonishing abode of mountain, plain, woodland, desert, jungle. Her waters restore and cleanse our bodies; her atmosphere gives us needed oxygen while shielding us from harmful ultraviolet rays; her minerals and vegetation provide us with an endless source and variety of foods.

Our connection to the earth remains unbroken throughout our lives. We are physically bound to her by gravity and by our need for oxygen, food, and water. Some people may consider their spiritual path to be found in efforts to leave the physical plane: to levitate, vacate the body, discover some other, "higher" realm of existence. They seem to be rejecting or denying their indissoluble tie with earth and matter. This could be a hazardous path; denying our connection with earth as source is splitting our worlds, not integrating them.

The story of Western civilization seems to be one of continuous effort to subdue nature and disconnect ourselves from our primal home, to become self-sufficient. We build cities, tear down forests, divert rivers, cover precious soil with concrete. We have forgotten our heritage, our source. The Native Americans have always recognized and honored their dependence upon Mother Earth. Their lives are conducted in partnership with the planet and her creatures. The most important knowledge the modern world can gain from its native peoples may be this neglected or forgotten truth. To be truly at home on our planet, to feel its nurturance, its bounteous goodness, its consciousness as a great living being, and to rest in harmonious relationship with that being—this is essential for our spiritual as well as for our physical survival and growth and evolution.

The music of the Mother is felt and heard and expressed in infinite ways. It is born of the silence of darkening clouds, in the dripping rain, in the thundering waterfall, in the river flowing into the ocean. If we could slow our own life processes sufficiently, we might detect the sounds of the seed bursting in the soil, the thrust of the grasses upward toward the sun, the unfolding of the flower. Within our own silence we might perceive the muffled, barely audible music of nature as it is born, grows, recedes, and dies.

Virtually all of the earth's creatures are music-makers: buzzing insects, howling mammals, and most notably, birds. Perhaps because flying creatures are able, for a time, to resist the pull of gravity, they can better tune in to the vibratory fields surrounding the planet. Maybe their songs serve to balance and harmonize the vibrations, thus feeding our spirits as the oxygen given off by plants feeds our breath. This may help explain the life-giving, health-promoting qualities of trees and birds.

Most of the rituals performed by native cultures are associated with nature. These rituals are accompanied by music: chanting, singing, playing rattles, flutes, drums. The use of music as a connection between the earth and its inhabitants has vanished from many cultures, but recently there has been renewed interest in joining ourselves with Mother Earth through music. We are playing our flutes for the dolphins and whales. We are celebrating the seasons and cycles of the Mother with rituals of music, poetry, drama, dance. The Western world is becoming more and more familiar with the music of the East, with sounds that imitate or emulate nature: the vina of India, the shakuhachi flute and koto of Japan.

In the music that we create, we can honor and renew our connection and relationship with Mother Earth. We can produce harmonious vibrations that link us with nature. By listening to the sounds of nature, we can bring these sounds into our minds and hearts and let them flow through our instruments. Thus we add our own unique music to that of the planet. In doing so, we are united with our sustenance and source—Mother Earth.

Exercise: Music and Nature

Go to a lovely spot in nature: the woods, the seashore, or a quiet spot of greenery in your own backyard. Sit quietly, gazing with soft eyes at the scene around you, at the sky, the earth, water, trees. Breathe in the odors. Feel the air on your skin. Feel the solidity of the ground on which you are sitting. Be aware of the direction and intensity of the sunlight, the shadowy places.

Now close your eyes and listen. With no judgment or definition or description, simply allow sound to flow into your body, not only through your ears, but also through your eyelids, hands, feet. Hear the sounds of Mother Earth breathing in and out of you as your breath moves in and out, up and down. Feel yourself being filled, permeated with the sounds.

Begin making gentle sounds of your own, sighing, humming, murmuring. Carry on a wordless conversation with the wind, the trees, the water, the insects and birds. Pause and listen for the response. Do not try to guess what is being communicated. Simply allow sounds to flow from your center outward and then wait for the sounds of nature to stream back into you. Gradually become aware of joining your sounds with those of your surroundings. Become one with nature, with Mother Earth, through sound.

A wonderful conversation may ensue on a warm summer evening as you join your voice with the melodies of the crickets. They will begin to chirp in perfect unison with your song.

You can also try this using a small instrument such as a flute, recorder, guitar, or drum.

The Primal Music

We are creatures of consciousness sheathed in the physical, mental, and emotional aspects of ourselves, existing in the present moment. While the only time that is real is now, we have emerged from a magical, mythical past in which our roots are still deeply embedded. This past is our point of origin, the matrix, the source. As the roots of a tree nourish and make possible the continued existence and growth of that tree, so we are sustained by our roots that extend deep into a forgotten reality. The aborigines of Australia call this past "dreamtime." It is not really the past but a different mode of reality in which our mythical selves exist concurrently with our ordinary everyday consciousness.

We may have forgotten our roots and deny that we are indeed linked with our beginnings in an indissoluble way. Modern, scientific man tends to want to believe he has left his primal self far in the past, that he has evolved from an ignorant, animalistic state to one of intellectual enlightenment. This illusion may be one of the major symptoms of our individual and social fragmentation. Our primal roots and mythical origins do not disappear or evolve. If they did, we would die, just as the tree with severed roots will die.

To discover our inherent wholeness, we must begin to recognize and accept our primal nature. As the planet grows ever smaller, the peoples of the so-called Third, Fourth and Fifth Worlds, the natives or "primitives," are attracting our attention. They are showing us parts of ourselves we have denied or forgotten. The revival of interest in the Native American consciousness is an indication that we are beginning to discover and to accept our primal nature.

We can contact our roots in the primal, mythical self through primal music. This may prove a challenge to our Western mind which may consider this type of music as simply pounding drums, repetitious drones, meaningless sounds that are not beautiful or even musical in our sense of the word. Primal music differs from the Western classical tradition in numerous ways, mirroring differences in the development of cultures and the corresponding development of individuals within those cultures. It encompasses the music of native tribes around the world; it is also deeply embedded in music composed and played today—music from East India, Indonesia, Persia, most of Asia, and much of Eastern Europe.

The essence of primal music is to be found in the total sound itself rather than in an orderly progression of tones in patterns of melody and harmony. Instead of melody, there is a line, a movement of tone, a stream of sound. There is a sense of timelessness, with no set beginning, middle, or end, and no fixed duration. There are few if any climaxes and resolutions, contrasts of loudness and softness, tensions and releases. Because of this, the listener is free to come into or move out of the musical experience at will. There are no focal points to attract the attention, but rather an air of symmetry inviting the listener to become one with the total sound. Thus the music does not manipulate the mind or emotions but engages the whole being in a clear but unfocussed total experience. Behind the outer sound, there throbs an inner pulse, touching the core, the essence of the hearer. It speaks strongly to the body; movement and dance play integral roles in the performance and appreciation of primal music.

Now that we are in communication with virtually all peoples on the planet, the music of all cultures is becoming available. A cross-cultural blend of many kinds of music is taking place, mirroring the acceptance and integration of our primal nature with other aspects of the self. As we are willing to experience the sounds of the gamelan orchestra of Indonesia, the drum choirs of Africa, the ragas of India, we are contacting our own source, our forgotten origins. We need to discover this neglected aspect of our being and lovingly integrate our mythical and our ordinary consciousness. This will bring us to an expanded awareness of our individual wholeness and also of our connection and oneness with all the peoples of the world.

Exercise: the Primal Music

1. Spend some time listening to music of other cultures: Eastern Indian, Chinese, Japanese, Indonesian, African, Native American. A wide variety of recordings is available. As you listen to a piece of primal music, stand with eyes closed. Feel the music throbbing within you. Begin moving or dancing. As

the music and movement end, feel the awakening that
has occurred in your body and your being.

2. Now if you have an instrument, take it up.
Feeling the vitality of your primal beingness, allow
that energy to flow through your instrument as
you play. The emerging music will be an expression
of your source, your mythical history. Play for a time
with awareness of your primal nature.

Beauty: Aesthetics

As human beings, we require beauty, we hunger for it, we watch and search for it. We cling to what we think is beautiful and mourn when it slips away from us. We attempt to define beauty through our personal or cultural preferences: prettiness, symmetry, sensuousness, inspirational qualities. We look for it in nature or in the faces of the people around us, and especially in the arts. When asked how we feel about a painting or a poem or a piece of music, our response is generally in terms of whether or not we think it is beautiful. "True" art seems to be that which expresses beauty.

While the need for beauty has always been with us, the science of aesthetics is a fairly recent concept in the exploration of beauty. When something is described as aesthetically pleasing—that is, beautiful —it is explained in terms of harmony, clarity, and symmetry. The tendency to describe beauty according to its outer qualities of color or line or rhythm may have begun in ancient Greece. The Greeks attempted to analyze and therefore to judge art through the use of mental concepts. Their ideas about beauty and its tie to aesthetics have predominated the Western mind for centuries. We have been attempting to explain or define beauty through psychological or sociological or historical approaches based upon what has gone before: the "laws" established by earlier artists. This method of judging what is beautiful has served music well: Mozart, Beethoven, Bach composed aesthetically superb works of art that inspire us with their harmony and order.

Beauty as aesthetics, however, is only a partial view. It is a mind-oriented and therefore judgmental vantage point that may often exclude other aspects of the perceptive process involved with the body, the emotions, the spirit. As we study nature, we see beauty in the gnarled oak tree bent by time and rain and wind, an ancient being whose endurance is proven in its twisted, weather-beaten form. We find beauty not only in the glowing silky skin of the infant but in the rough, rutted face of the aged. The dandelion is as beautiful as the rose, the vulture as the robin, when mind judgments are suspended. The so-called dissonances of modern music, the nonmetric, assymmetrical rhythms, the unexplained silences— these too are beautiful.

A more complete, unerring beauty may be discovered as we look for the wholeness inherent in all forms and try to find the true physical and spiritual nature of its manifestation. Whatever speaks from and to and about that wholeness we may call beautiful. Whatever moves us into an expanded awareness of the totality of our beingness is beautiful. Beauty is more than prettiness or pleasure-giving or established order; it is majesty, grandeur, wholeness, a mirror of the cosmos and of the Self. We experience beauty as we listen to music that addresses and engages our whole being. This experience connects our inner and outer worlds and brings us to an awareness of our inherent wholeness, within and without.

We need not throw out the whole concept of aesthetics. But it is important to realize that it is simply that: a concept, a mind construct, and therefore at best a partial view. A more complete experience of beauty is available through the senses and feelings, through the body and spirit, as well as through the mind. As we are open and eager to search for beauty with new eyes and a larger heart, with our total being, we fulfill a greater purpose for the music we hear and compose and perform: that of bringing ourselves and others to an increased awareness of our inherent wholeness, an awareness of Self. Therein lies true beauty.

Exercise: Beauty, Aesthetics

With art materials at hand, listen to a piece of music that you consider particularly beautiful. Begin painting or drawing or sculpting as the music plays. Leave aside critical thought, silencing *all* thought as much as possible. Simply play with the art, creating as you listen. When the music ends, put your art work aside.

Now play some music you do not think is beautiful at all, something you dislike intensely. Create something with the art materials using a different medium such as pastels rather than watercolors or clay instead of pencil and paper. When the music ends, examine the art you created. Compare it with the earlier work. Which is more pleasing? Which moves you? Which is beautiful?

Listen to each piece of music a second time, looking at your art as the music plays.

54

Spend some time with something that you do not consider beautiful. It may even be repulsive to you. As you look, observe without judgment any emotions that may arise. Allow the apparent ugliness of the object to reveal to you an inherent wholeness. See if you can remain with it until you begin to perceive some beauty in it. Even decaying garbage has a kind of beauty, in the astounding way that micro-organisms cause it to disintegrate.

Inner Music

Our physical world is one of duality. There is an outer and inner reality to all that we are and experience. Our exterior world depends upon the inner life: the source, the pivotal point or axis upon which our outer lives revolve. For those who are conscious of only the purely materialistic realms, there is little or no awareness of the source of life, the center. They know of no inner reality; life seems to consist solely of physical matter and temporal events. They live somewhere out on the periphery of things, attempting to shape and control their world at its outer edges rather than from the center. Enormous amounts of energy are consumed and mostly wasted as they attempt to turn the wheel of existence at the rim rather than at the axis.

As we evolve in consciousness, we become more aware of the powerful truth that the outer world is created, affected, moved, changed by that which is at the center: an unseen, unheard but nonetheless real force. There are endless paths into the center of our being. Meditation is perhaps the most widely known technique consciously applied for this purpose. The arts, especially music, are elements of the outer physical world that are most obviously connected with the inner world of spirit. Playing or listening to music can bring us to our inner reality in an instant. It is as though a golden cord extends from the spiritual, nonmaterial essence at our center out into the world of corporeality where music exists in space and time and audibility.

Music, then, is a concrete, physical link with the nonmaterial spirit. It is a space where outer and inner meet, correcting our misperceptions about duality and separation. It brings matter and spirit into a oneness with no boundaries. There is a music that exists in the outer world of sound, tone, rhythm, and volume. The same music is playing within us in the lungs, the blood, the cells. Even in the atoms of the body a dance of electrons and protons and neutrons is creating music and at the same time responding to its own inner music. If our physical senses were fully developed, we might hear this music and feel this dance. As it is, we must use the outer sound as a mirror or reflection of the music within.

All this may sound poetic and fanciful, but if we are to take the idea of a spiritual reality seriously, we must conclude that that inner world is alive, real, and musical. There can be no outer existence without its inner counterpart; there is no music "out there" in the world of audibility that does not also reside within the center in that unseen reality at the core of the universe, the Self.

As we begin to acknowledge our inner worlds, we can start using music as a conscious guide to reach those worlds. We can begin to allow the illusionary boundaries between the physical and the spiritual to dissolve. The duality of the illusory world where separation seems to exist becomes one reality, whole and complete. The outer music fades and dies; its echoes linger at the center. The inner music tells us we are spirit.

Exercise: Inner Music

1. Sit in silence, eyes closed. Listen for the inaudible inner sounds of your being. Imagine music playing within. This is not memory or mind work but real listening.

As you begin to perceive sound within, start moving to that music. Allow the silent music to play your body as an instrument.

Observe without judgment any feelings and thoughts that may arise; let them flow through you and be expressed by your movement.

At some point you may hear or feel the inner sound fading away. Then rest in the silence.

2. With your voice or instrument, begin to imitate the inner music you heard and moved with. If you heard nothing, express that nothingness as audible sound. Acknowledge the emerging music as an outer expression of the music within.

II

The Musician

The Player

Everyone has the gift of music; it is intrinsic to our nature. No one is separate from music; it is within all of us as well as outside us. We are all musicians, receivers and players of vibration and pulse and motion and silence. We orchestrate our lives and, to the extent we are in touch with our inner being, we use music to create a rich and fulfilling existence.

What makes a musician? The special God-given talent with which one is born? Years of study and practice? Determination coupled with great enthusiasm for the art of music? All these are contributing factors. But the reality still remains that all of us are inherently musicians. We need simply to honor this truth and move with it.

Many people, nonmusicians in particular, dispute this view. They feel the musician is exceptional, gifted. They see musicians as a breed apart, special, favored, more fortunate than most. There is some truth in this incomplete view. Musicians are exceptional in the sense that they willingly and lovingly receive the gift available to all. They have taken what is offered, magnified it, made it their own. The classical musician of India may study and practice for as long as twenty years before being considered ready to perform. Most classical musicians in any culture have a background of many years of intensive study. There are others, however, who are completely self-taught; their devotion to music has opened them to use the gift we all have.

The child responds to sounds while still in the womb. This response continues and intensifies as she is born into the physical realm of vibration and rhythm. The newly born infant does not distinguish boundaries between herself and the rest of the world; she carries within her an innate knowledge of the oneness of all being. Soon she finds that the oneness can be broken: the mother leaves the room, the finger she grasps is pulled away. But sounds, unlike touch or visual images, remain within her. It may be some time before she conceives of sound as something apart from herself.

This connection may never have been broken for musicians. Although our rational, logical, reasoning minds deduce that the music we hear is emanating from stereo speakers across the room, something deep within, some prenatal, primordial sense, tells us that the sound is a part of us, not separate. The awareness of our own musicianship may lie in this knowledge.

The role of musicians in modern society is an exalted one: they are admired and often envied by those who do not sing, compose, or play an instrument. Oddly enough, financial support is not always included as a measure of that esteem. Our society's priorities center on the technological aspects of life rather than on the nonmaterial, unmeasurable, fluid world of music.

In older societies everyone participated in music.

All of the tribespeople sang and danced and composed sacred songs that were directly concerned with their everyday existence. In the Native American culture, an individual's prosperity was assessed by the number of songs the person composed or "owned." There were some who may have been recognized as having special talents and abilities, but they were not set apart as elite members of society. Music and the musicians were an integral part of life.

The decision to be a musician, to use music as the primary vehicle for one's journey through this life, generally is made at an early age. Somehow one feels one has always wanted to be a musician. Perhaps it would be more natural and healthier to be unaware of choices, allowing music to flow into one's being freely, without conscious decisions about if or when or how it will happen.

Musicians are intimately in touch with all aspects of their being: the physical body, essential for making music; the emotions, for there is no music without feeling; the mind, which masters the technicalities of the notes and the instrument; and the spirit, that unbroken tie with the inner being. Music collects all the seemingly disparate parts of the musician and brings them into oneness, wholeness.

For some this wholeness is experienced on an unconscious level: musicians feel most healthy and happiest while playing music, without understanding or even caring why. As they become aware of the ways in which music is making them whole, they begin to expand that circle of wholeness to include others and, ultimately, all of life. Music then becomes a spiritual practice, which means bringing the spirit into every aspect of one's being and consciously expressing that spirit in every musical experience.

Exercise: The Player

Choose a recording of music that is not descriptive. It may be sounds rather than organized tones, such as Tibetan bells, shakuhachi flute, meditation music.

As the music plays, sit with eyes closed. You are going to recall the first time you experienced music. As the sound stirs this memory within you, allow it to flow through you. Let your hands move to the memory, choreographing that memory in space.

This act of recalling is not a thought process, but rather a recollection at a deeper level. As such, it may or may not have a recognizable form that could be expressed as thought. When the music ends, sit in silence and gratitude. (Adapted from Carolyn Kenny's workshop)

The Physical Realm

We live as physical beings in a physical world, a
world of matter, substance, form. We are grounded by
the force of gravity. We are tied to the earth by the
body's needs for oxygen, water, food. We are limited
and bound by our physical universe. Through the
wonders of modern technology, we can travel out into
space beyond the gravitational field. But the ultimate
boundary of the physical realm, the mortality of
the body, has not been dissolved.

The world of matter is an obvious one. Our senses
see light, hear sound, taste and touch the solid stuff of
which the world seems to be composed. But scientists,
particularly physicists, have discovered that the
world our senses describe is not the real world.
Matter, it turns out, is not solid. It is particles or waves
or simply some sort of energy vibrating at high speeds
in space as vast and empty as that of the heavens.
The illusoriness of the material world as viewed by
the spiritual traditions of the East is being cor-
roborated by the Western scientific community. The
relevance of Eastern spirituality to Western materiality has been a revelation for spiritual seekers. It
seems to invite us to follow the path of the Hindus

65

and Buddhists who insist that we are not the visible body but spirit. The insubstantiality of matter seen through scientific eyes brings us nearer to the Eastern ideal of living in the physical world as non-physical beings.

We might ask why we should inhabit physical bodies in a world of matter at all. If our goal is to discover our essense or spirit, of what use is the physical body? The goal of realizing spirit might lead us to pray, to meditate, even to levitate in an attempt to block out the physical world in order to contact spirit. The body may be at best a somewhat cumbersome vehicle to carry out the ideas of the mind, or at worst an enemy that becomes hungry, overweight, ill, a thwarter of the concepts of the higher aspects of mind and spirit.

In truth, we are as much our bodies as we are our minds. The same stuff—the protons and electrons and neutrons dancing within the cells of the liver and heart and lungs—is also performing in the neurons of the brain. Within the past decade or two, physicists and biologists have been making astounding break-throughs in their pursuit of answers to the question: What is life? The discovery of the DNA helix provides us with an explanation for the orderly continuation of life forms from one generation to the next. Physicists are beginning to speak of the eternal electron: energy detectable as a wave or particle moving in its own random way. Subatomic particles may even be said to have choice, or "free will"; as such they may have intelligence and consciousness. Some scientists believe that the electron is a micro-cosm of the black hole in space: a field of energy in which time and space as we know it are reversed.*

As we view the physical world in this new way, we become aware of the essential unity of our own beingness. The nonmaterial energy of electrons and subatomic particles is in no way separate and apart from the objects of the physical world. Similarly, spirit and matter are one at every level: cellular, molecular, atomic. Each of the tens of billions of electrons making up the body is also spirit, as spirit is also matter, energy. As we see this basic unity, this no-boundary world of intermingling, unified physical and spiritual universes, the purpose of our physical bodies becomes clear: without matter there can be no spirit. To reach the world of spirit, we have the physical realm to guide us. To delve into the physical world is to discover spirit.

In order to become one with something, all sense of separateness must be abandoned. To become one with the physical body, we must dissolve the barriers set up by the mind conditioned either by Eastern spirituality or Western materiality. Children are innately one with their bodies, perhaps because they are still in touch with their eternal nature as both spiritual and physical beings.

It is particularly important for the musician to be aware of being a unity of matter and spirit, rather than focusing on a relationship between the two. The whole body is engaged while playing music: the limbs, the breath, the ears, the senses of touch and balance. The result of this physical engagement

---

*For a detailed discussion of these ideas, see Jean E. Charon, *The Unknown Spirit* (London: Coventure Ltd., 1983) and Jeremy W. Hayward, *Perceiving Ordinary Magic* (Boulder, Colo.: Shambhala, 1984).

is sound or vibration, a physical phenomena. As this sound emanates, an invisible energy goes forth as spirit. Boundaries dividing matter and spirit fade and dissolve as the music pours forth as wholeness, oneness. As musicians become conscious of the process, they are exalted. They move into that state called heaven on earth, for if there is such a thing as heaven, it is the realm of nonduality. The heaven the mystics seek is available here and now in this physical realm when musicians play their instruments and pour out into the world the physical/ spiritual Self.

Exercise: The Physical Realm

1. This is a body-awareness technique. Choose a recording of gentle, flowing music, perhaps a quiet raga played on an Indian flute. Lie comfortably on the floor, eyes closed, breathing softly. As the music begins, imagine that the music is water flowing all around you, that you are floating on a sea of sound. Feel the weightlessness, the buoyancy of your body. Allow the music to cradle you gently and safely.

When you feel very relaxed, imagine the music slowly, peacefully entering your body through the soles of your feet. Feel the sound vibrations moving into your feet; put your full attention there. This is not a mental kind of attention but rather sensual. Become aware of the shape, temperature, mass, contours of your feet as the music draws your attention there. Let the music remain there for as long as you like.

When you are ready, feel the music flowing through your legs, again with all your senses attending to this area of your body. Feel the music slowly flowing through your knees, your thighs, your pelvis, your torso, your back. Let it flow into your arms and hands, upward into your head, always with sensual awareness of the part of your body in which the music is flowing.

As the music ends, observe your whole body. Feel its heightened sensitivity as you have placed your awareness upon it.

2. Now play the same music again. This time, however, begin moving with it. Let your body make all choices of movement. The music is within you and will move you without thought or effort on the part of the conscious mind. The mind is simply the observer, not interfering, nonjudgmental, detached. Feel your reality as a body filled with and moving to the music.

As the sound stops, remain in the silence, allowing the vibrations to continue in the spaciousness of your cells.

The World of Feeling

The most immediate connection between our inner selves and the outer world of relationship is made through our feelings. Our ability to relate to others depends upon our acknowledgment, acceptance, and expression of feelings. In this technological, head-oriented society, the tendency has been to negate, suppress or ridicule feelings. However, having brought ourselves to the brink of global annihilation, many of us are finally beginning to question the currently accepted ideology of intellectual supremacy over feelings and emotions.

One aspect of Woman (or the feminine principle when it is equal with or dominant over the masculine principle in either sex) is to be in contact with her feeling nature. In Western society, we have tended to suppress this half of the self, which is nurturing, caring, receptive, emotional. As both sexes move toward a balance of masculine and feminine aspects, there is a corresponding expansion in our awareness of and expression of feeling. Since we are most intimately connected with each other through feelings, the consciousness of our oneness is thus enhanced.

70

A major barrier to the acknowledgment and acceptance of feelings is the mental judgments we place upon them: love is good, anger is bad; pain is negative, pleasure is positive; fear is terrible, excitement is wonderful. Feelings, however, unhindered by our judgments about them, simply *are*: not good, bad, desirable, undesirable, worthy, or unworthy. It is the mind that creates problems with feelings. When we realize this, we have removed the first great block to our connection with our feeling nature.

Feelings are our teachers. Because they are expressions of our inchoate, invisible nature, they tell us about ourselves. We generally tend to view our feelings as reactions or responses to persons or circumstances outside ourselves. In the sense that we are all connected, all one, this is true. At the same time, though, those events and persons "out there" are really mirrors reflecting, through our feelings about them, our own inner nature. Feelings of envy or anger or admiration or love tell us little about the person who aroused them but a lot about who we are. When we can begin owning our feelings, taking responsibility for them, recognizing the very personal nature of our feeling world, then we are ready to listen to our feelings and to be instructed and enlightened by them.

A Course in Miracles states that there are only two kinds of communication: we are either giving love or we are asking for love. While this may seem an oversimplification, to categorize our feelings in this way may be helpful in understanding and accepting them and in bringing ourselves into wholeness through them. When I feel angry, what part of me is asking for love? How can I give myself the love needed to dissolve that anger? It may not be necessary

71

or even helpful to analyze our feelings; when the mind is engaged, blockage may occur. To search in the past for sources of anger may be helpful for some. But dealing with the feeling here and now, in the present moment (the only moment in which we can act), requires the relinquishment of past and future. Being with the anger now, feeling its movement and energy as a tangible presence, may carry us to that part of ourselves that feels unloved. And when we reach that space, we may have to simply be there, sit for awhile in that place of unlovingness. We can begin to deal with such feelings only there because that is their source.

We have the choice of whether or not we acknowledge this place of source. We can choose to nurture our feelings, honor their validity, allow their expression, which brings us to a greater awareness of our wholeness; or we may deny and avoid the source, causing fragmentation and subsequent suffering.

Sometimes when we decide to get in touch with our feelings, so-called negative emotions arise—anger, sorrow, fear, pain—and we want to shut them out. But this will not make them disappear. We simply waste energy with our efforts to suppress them. By allowing all feeling, "good" and "bad," to be experienced, a great source of energy is made available.

Many feelings arise out of a judgmental attitude, but in the end the person we are judging is the self. When we stop judging our feelings, we can get a fairly clear look at our inner psyche—our fear, love, sorrow, joy. When we find someone or something that brings us great pleasure, then we are in touch with the aspects of ourselves that we accept and love. But our dislikes and negative feelings tell us the most and lead us to those unacceptable parts of ourselves that we cannot allow to surface.

Emotions are our inner feelings moving outwards. As such, they become vehicles for great energy. Without that energy informing them, our actions are sterile, uncommitted, and often meaningless.

In experiencing music, it is important to allow feelings and emotions full rein. The habitually judging mind can block the flow of feeling. This not only prevents our really hearing the music but also blocks our view of our inner nature. Great music can serve as a clear, polished surface, a mirror of the inner feeling self.

Music has the unique power to bring us to an awareness of our feelings in an unfettered way. Somehow it is acceptable to shed tears while listening to a Mahler symphony, the same tears we suppress when confronted with our own or another's pain. Music informs us that we are creatures of feeling, that our feelings are valid, that there is nothing wrong about experiencing them. For some people, one of the few conscious connections they have with their feelings may come through listening to music. So musicians have a sacred responsibility to honor the power of music; to recognize the inviolate nature of another's feelings; to refuse to manipulate those feelings. They must remain ever aware of the penetrating power of their art in reaching the innermost spaces of the human heart.

Exercise: The World of Feeling

We often experience feeling in a very physical, sensual way, and it is closely connected with our breathing. Thus holding the breath is the most effective way of shutting off feeling. Strong emotions, when allowed to be felt, change the rhythm and depth of one's breathing; conversely, the deepening and speeding up of the breath can evoke strong emotion. When you feel a particularly intense emotion arising, watch your breath: observe the way in which it seems to quicken, to become shallow and uneven. Take deep, slow, even breaths, imagining that the feeling is moving on the air as it passes in and out of the body.

When you are experiencing an especially intense emotion, whether sadness or joy or anger, immediately turn on your tape recorder and begin expressing your emotion through sound: crying, laughing, screaming, singing, or playing an instrument. It may be a series of unconnected sounds or a simple melody, whatever will allow the full rein of expression of your feelings.

Let your voice carry you to the source of the feeling. Allow the sounds to touch and move that part of you in which the feeling resides. If you feel it as a physical place in the body, observe the sensations in that area. Let your sounds stay with the feeling at its source as long as it is comfortable to do so.

Later, when the intensity of feeling has lessened, you may wish to listen to the recording. Try moving to the sounds you produced, recreating the feeling in memory. You may want to do some art work, providing a visual image of a deep feeling.

Musician as Creator

We create our own world. We have largely chosen our physical reality: the degree of health we enjoy; our environment or the space in which we live and work and play; our employment; our pleasures; our habits and desires. Our world of relationships flows and fluctuates as we attract others who are like us, reflecting our acknowledged selves, and those who are unlike us, the "difficult" ones who can teach us. We create our own psychological, emotional, intellectual climate as we respond to or react to our encounters with the world. We may even have created the circumstances of our birth, the incarnating soul being aware of, and so choosing, the kind of life needed for its ongoing evolution.

When we act without awareness, we are unconsciously creating future consequences of those acts through karma. Most of us have spent vast time spans, whole lifetimes, accruing and then working out karma. Our unconscious actions are vividly reflected in our life situations, in our health, in our relationships, if only we could see.

At some point we begin to awaken. Awareness of our nature as spirit, of our role as co-creator of self and universe, dawns. Like the petals of the flower opening to the sun, we become increasingly aware of the light without and within us. At this moment of opening, we start making conscious choices and recognizing and accepting responsibility for those choices. Our creations begin to enhance growth and evolution, to make us aware of our inherent wholeness and of our oneness with all of life. As we discover our own creative role, a spaciousness occurs in our lives. We begin seeing others as co-creators, and a new kind of relationship based on respect and reverence and love develops. The burden of placing responsibility or blame on others is lifted. We discover the delightful freedom of our own creativity.

The creative life is related to the spiritual life. To contact, acknowledge, and utilize our creative energy awakens us to our core, our essence. When we examine the qualities of creative people—musicians, artists, chefs, poets—we discover that their attributes are often similar to those of mystics. In many cases, consciously developing creative aspects of the self awakens spiritual potentialities as well.

Many truly creative people—Beethoven and van Gogh, for instance—may not seem to embody these attributes. It is possible to be creative without being spiritually perfect, of course. But as we look at the qualities of the ideal creative person, we may discover deeper and richer possibilities for our own creative expression than we had ever imagined. No one person will express all of these qualities, but everyone who is creative will show some of them. Together these attributes and attitudes suggest an ideal to which we can aspire.

One attribute of many consciously creative people is openness to the present moment. With ever-increasing clarity, they see the totality, the perfection of the Now. They accept this moment as the only reality. Unbounded by past regrets or future probabilities, they are free to explore all the possibilities here, now. They are unafraid and so can afford to take risks. For them there is no such concept as what might be or what might have been because everything is already happening in the Now—a complete moment.

Creative people also tend to be confident of their abilities. As with mystics, they are in touch with the Source. They recognize that Source as the matrix and fount of creativity and, in a sense, give over responsibility to something beyond themselves. Their goal is to become an ever clearer channel for the expression of all that flows from whatever source inspires their creativity.

A lightness is present in some creative persons. This manifests as a sort of childlike wonder, good humor, cheerfulness, the feeling that life, while sacred, is not serious. There is present a wise energy, enthusiasm tempered by compassion.

Creative people are visionary. They see things that "aren't there" in the physical, material sense. They are aware of the inner workings of outer phenomena. Many pay attention to their daydreams and night dreams. Some understand the significance of myths and find their personal myths by which they may be guided. They can then allow their myths to alter or dissolve as life changes.

Another attribute of some creative people is to be flowing, fluid, aware of life's inherent motion. These people are utterly willing to move with and surrender to that motion without resistance. They are unattached to results or goals. They see patterns and work with them. They recognize the paradoxical nature of life and live with it, enjoy it, rather than feeling frustrated by it. They are nonprogrammed and spontaneous.

Creative people love some form of beauty, although their idea of it may not be the conventional one. They tend to see beauty everywhere, knowing that their vision of the outer world is a reflection of the beauty present within themselves. They embody the feminine aspects of receptivity and patience. They might see themselves as incubators in which creative impulses are lovingly nurtured and from which their creations will emerge.

Often creative people who are more spiritually oriented feel the spaciousness, the boundlessness, of themselves and of the cosmos. They might experience themselves as energy in larger energy fields and feel space and energy flowing in and around and through them. Some are in touch with the mystical. Edvard Grieg once said, "We composers are projections of the infinite into the finite." Those in touch with this dimension tend to have a deep reverence for life and see relationships among all things. They feel their own connection with all beings. They continually move toward wholeness within themselves, in their creations, and in the world. They might experience time cyclically rather than chronologically, seeing life's journey as a leaving and returning, not as a beginning with a middle and an end.

Creators are never separate from their creations. Musicians remain one with their music. This is obvious during the incubation period when the music is being dreamed about, felt but unexpressed. The music is the unborn child in the womb of the mother. As sound emerges into the worlds of space and time and listeners, musicians may feel that the music is leaving them, separating from them. But we are never separate from our creations. When we can feel our oneness with our outbound music, we can feel our oneness with our entire created world. As we create our lives, so we are also created by those around us, inextricably united with them in a whole and sacred manner.

Exercise: Musician as Creator

1. Choose an object in your home that you consider particularly beautiful. It may be a creation of your own or someone else's. Spend some time just looking at it.
Now select a recording of music that somehow seems to complement the object. (Debussy is a perfect match for a lovely water-color painting I have.) While listening to the music, feast your eyes on the object. When the music ends, begin writing, painting, drawing—in some way expressing whatever the experience of looking and listening has opened within you. Later you may want to listen to the music again as you look at what you created. Poetry written while listening to a certain piece of music acquires added dimension and beauty if it is read to that same music.

2. Upon awakening in the morning, start singing, or go immediately to your instrument and begin playing. Allow yourself to remain in your nighttime consciousness; feel as though you are playing in a dream. If you recall fragments of dreams, play or sing them. Continue until you have made a complete transition to waking consciousness.
If you have been recording your music, listen to the tape. Dance or draw or write as your night music plays.

Finding Our Myths

Life can be seen as a mythic journey in which the destination lies within. All events, relationships, manifestations in the outer world can be vehicles or symbols that transport us to the center of our being. This is the basis of the symbolic life—the bringing of the self to the Self.

A myth has been described as something that never was yet is always happening. It narrates a sacred history, a true history because it always deals with realities. Therefore, it can supply models for human behavior. According to Joseph Campbell, noted authority on myths, a myth has four essential functions. First, it elicits and supports a sense of awe before the mystery of life. Second, it portrays a cosmology, an image of the universe that supports this sense of awe. Third, myths support the current social order, integrating the individual organically into society. Finally, myth can help initiate the individual into the realities of the psyche.

To know the myths is to understand the beginnings, how things came to be, the story of creation. The sacred birth is the start of the mythical journey. The characters in myths are larger than life, but they are true images of our own reality.

In earlier, more primitive times, individuals lived in close relationship with the rest of society. This relationship was acknowledged, defined, and recreated periodically through the performance of rituals designed to show the sacred connections between people and to bring them to an awareness of their own personal stories. Through ritual and myth, individuals were able to identify with their archetypes, providing them with a view of themselves and their place in the cosmos. Because of the multiplicity of choices in our modern society, our vagabond life styles often take us far from our roots. It is difficult for us to relate to a single group myth as found in primitive societies.

Yet we all have personal myths. They are maps of consciousness and the containers of many levels of knowledge. We create our myths by condensing and focusing energies; these energies can be released throughout our mythic journey, aiding us in the consummation of our life's purpose. We may do this by creating a ritual of some sort that reminds us of, connects us with, and celebrates a particular myth. For example, we may portray the cycles of the seasons through music, movement, poetry, or art. In a way, we are reliving the story, discovering our personal identity with it, and creating a physical manifestation of our own cyclic nature. By discovering our myths, we emerge from linear, chronological time and enter a different space and time—a sacred time, dreamtime.

To find our way on this mythic journey, we need to provide our own symbols and our own myths, and we need to discover ways to connect them to the ancient, eternal archetypes. Through this process of discovery and connection of our symbols with archetypes, a core of meaning for our individual lives begins to emerge. Until we have an awareness of who it is that is taking the journey, why it is necessary, and some sense of its destination, life will seem empty, incomplete, meaningless. Myths offer one way to find meaning in life.

We can create our myths and symbols in various ways. We can study the archetypes, such as the shadow, the anima and animus, death and rebirth, the spiral, the mandala, the trickster, the perilous journey, looking for correlations between such expressions of the collective unconscious and our own being. We may record and examine our dreams, searching for the myriad meanings to be found within the unconscious mind. We can probe our feelings through music, art, poetry, drama, movement and find images, sounds, words, and other physical expressions that resonate with our own being. We may explore our artistic creations as symbols of our inner being. We may consciously connect with others through service or teaching or relationship, thereby discovering their symbols. Then we are able to relate their myths, their journeys, to our own. We may see in all our experiences symbols that point to meaning and hints of where our journey is leading.

The arts may provide the most obvious and accessible purveyors of myth and meaning. Painting, sculpture, drama, dance, music have been vehicles for the expression of the symbolic life since the beginning of time. Some anthropologists say that song may have predated speech as a conveyor of meaning. We cannot know the quality or extent of language at the time when imaginative, beautiful images were being painted on the walls of caves. Meaningful movement or pantomime may have been a highly developed skill before language was in use.

Pure music is the most unalloyed expression of meaning because it does not depict or portray anything other than itself: the meaning is intrinsic to the sound. The sound is the symbol, connecting us with our own meanings. We may intellectually link a Strauss waltz with a historical period in time or to an image of couples floating in an elegant ballroom. But the music itself, removed from its historical background, is just motion—rhythmic, vibrant, melodic. It connects us with the flowing, rhythmic nature of our own being. This is the true symbolic role of music: that of making us aware—through our senses, feelings, and body—of our own mythic reality.

Through our musical preferences and our identification with particular modes of music, we can become aware of our inner story, the sacred history we are living. Our choices provide clues to our personal myths as we are receptive, nonjudgmental, and conscious of which music moves us to ask who we are. When we experience music in this way, we create and live out the myths that provide energy and meaning and a sense of holiness for our existence.

Exercise: Finding Our Myths

1. Make a list of your ten all-time favorite pieces of music. Choosing one selection each day, sing or play or listen to that piece as often as possible, observing the thoughts, feelings, and memories that emerge. After you have spent a day with each of the ten selections, see if you can discover a single thread of meaning connecting them.

2. Before falling asleep at night, mentally review the day just ending. Recall events, feelings, thoughts

in as much detail as possible. The following morning, begin singing or go to your instrument and begin playing, allowing any dreams or fragments of dreams to emerge through the music. See if you can discover correlations between your dreams and yesterday's journey. Allow the events and feelings of the preceding day's story to relate to one another in mythical form through your music.

The Musician and the Shadow

We live in a world of duality: masculine and feminine, yin and yang, matter and spirit, light and shadow. We can only guess at the reasons for this, but we recognize the necessity of reconciling the dichotomies, of somehow bringing the opposites into balance and, ultimately, into wholeness and oneness.

Each individual is a microcosm, a holographic image of the macrocosm that is the universe. As polarities appear in the cosmos, so they are also present in us. It is easier to discover and observe duality outside ourselves because as human, physical beings we appear self-contained, complete, whole. However, in reality, we view the world in exactly the same way that we see ourselves: when the outer world seems fragmented and filled with paradox and unreconcilable opposites, we are looking at a reflection of our view of our own inner being. When we begin to accept our model of the universe as an image of the self, everything and everyone can become our teachers, our guides to self-knowledge.

Some aspects of ourselves are readily recognizable to us and to others. Our most obvious identity has been by gender (although recently the distinctions are becoming blurred as both sexes express more of the opposite polarity). I am woman; I have identified myself in this way from my earliest memories. This is readily apparent. I am also, somewhere within, masculine. That realization can be difficult to deal with, a paradox too complex for ordinary awareness to reconcile. And so it remains in the shadows, resisting the light of consciousness.

Light and shadow move and shift and play within us. For many, the shadowy parts feel threatening, heavy, foreboding. We cannot allow the light to shine on these phantoms; we feel that they are somehow shameful and not to be looked upon. And so we project them out upon the world onto people, events, nations, even onto our pets. We are then able to react to our projections with anger, fear, hatred, sometimes with envy—in any but loving ways—as though they are something outside us. We cannot own our shadows, and they threaten us from the recesses of our unconscious mind. We repudiate them because we have not learned that they are as essential to our being as shadow is to sunlight or as matter is to spirit. We are unable to understand that without our shadowy hidden side, we cannot be whole.

How can we discover our shadows? By observing our resistances. We may feel resistance to another person, to another's ideas or ideology, or to an alternate view of reality. We may feel repugnance for a life style different from our own. The resistance may seem valid and ethical—an abhorrence of violence or a fear of death—or it may be illogical, such as a strong revulsion to cats. These are our unowned shadows, fragments of the psyche seeking discovery and acceptance. The more vehement the resistance, the more deeply hidden is that aspect of our inner world. Since we can bring our shadows into the light by seeing their reflections in the world, we should perhaps be grateful for the mirrors put before us. "Love your enemies" will benefit not only our foes but, more profoundly, ourselves.

Watch for your resistances; study them, embrace them. They are spiritual guides. Although we may refuse to look at our shadows, the act of embracing, becoming one with our resistances will shed light upon the dark regions within. To accept anger or fear or violence as one's own, engendered not by the "other" but from within oneself, is the beginning of wholeness.

Music helps us meet our resistances courageously and almost in spite of our unwillingness to do so. Because it is fluid and moving, music streams into us and we flow with it, even against our conscious will. Our bodies are naturally so in tune with the sound and rhythm of music that it takes a stubborn intellect to resist.

When we find resistance to certain kinds of music, it is worth observing what it is that we are pushing against. The relentless beat of hard rock may be touching the primal self we feel we have evolved out of. The seemingly boring, repetitive sounds of an Indian raga may be moving us unwillingly out of our critical, judgmental intellectuality. The clang of the gamelan orchestra may be telling us that life is fuller, richer, less orderly than our concepts of harmony define. The insipid, watered-down elevator Muzak may be echoing something within ourselves that also feels somehow diluted and unnecessary and unfaithful to our own truth.

In the moist warm darkness of the earth, a seed

bursts and begins to grow. With patience and time, as it receives nourishment, it eventually reaches out into the sunlight, moving its stems and branches and leaves upward to realize the fullness of its being. Its roots remain in the darkness receiving food and water for continued growth. Even if we accept our shadows and cast the light of consciousness upon them, parts of ourselves may never reach the sunlight but remain hidden, nourishing us in secret ways that are directly and essentially connected to the fulfillment of our evolutionary cycle.

We are free to choose those aspects or our being we wish to bring into the light and those which will, at least for the time being, remain in shadow. Our resistances to our so-called "enemies" are telling us which elements are reaching for illumination; heeding these signals will bring us into a greater awareness of our inherent wholeness.

"Embrace the enemy, for he is us." His message is clear for those who will listen: "I am you. Recognize me; accept and enfold me; become one with me; become one with yourself."

Exercise: The Musician and the Shadow

This exercise requires two other participants: a movement partner and someone to accompany you on an instrument. A large gong is ideal; a conga or any good-sized drum will do. For a few days, carefully observe your resistances: an individual, a nation, an event, whatever arouses annoyance or anger. Choose one of these persons or situations to be portrayed in this shadow play.

Stand or sit facing your partner. She is your shadow

and will mirror every move you make. As the gong or drum begins sounding, allow yourself to become that which you resist. Take as long as you need to begin feeling yourself as that person or situation. Begin moving as that which you have resisted; immerse yourself fully in the role. Quietly, softly, without judgment, observe your feelings, thoughts, and body movements as you see yourself mirrored by your partner, your shadow.

Exchange places with the accompanying musician and with your shadow partner in turn, providing each of them the opportunity to participate in the shadow play.

The Musician and Transformation

The key to evolution is transformation. While we live in a world of movement and flow, there are certain experiences that bring about sudden and lasting alterations in our lives. Transformation is such a radical change involving our total being.

The metamorphosis of the butterfly presents us with an example from the biological world of the stark, dramatic changes that occur in the process called transformation. An earthbound caterpillar turns into a beautiful winged creature with virtually no resemblance to its earlier form. During the metamorphosis from caterpillar to adult, all the caterpillar's organs are melted, liquified, providing energy for the next stage of development. Nothing remains of the earlier form.

The process of transformation of the human psyche is no less extreme. While the ultimate physical metamorphosis occurs at the time of death when the body itself disintegrates, transformation of the being, the soul, the self can happen at any point in one's life, revealing the true Self.

The process is not without pain. Any change may cause discomfort; the more dramatic and rapid the change, the more pain may be involved. In the transformation of consciousness we must be willing to die to our former selves, no lesser event to deal with than our eventual physical demise. We experience resistance, attachment, anger, fear, and bereavement for our loss of the old. There is a feeling of emptiness, of nothingness, as the former self melts before the newly transformed being is fully established.

Fear of the unknown makes us resist transformation; we do not want it, we're content with things as they are. But evolution is inevitable; it is an intrinsic part of the cosmos. We may protest and resist, but growth and evolution of consciousness go on. As we can accept and surrender to the necessity of the process and are willing to flow gently with the stream of life in its fullness, the change can come about. We can become winged creatures with our boundaries dissolved. We can exist in a mode of being that is utterly new, evolved, enlightened, free. We discover that the pain, in retrospect, has been relatively brief and surprisingly bearable. Later we may recall the time of transformation as a period of excitement, of terror, of wonder.

Astonishing things can happen as we assent to our own metamorphosis. When we surrender to the painful loss of the old being, our hearts open wide to accept and welcome not only our own suffering, but the suffering of the world as well. This can carry us to the joyful realization that we are truly one with all beings. There may be no better way to experience unity with all life than through our willingness to accept and feel our own pain.

In helping initiate a global transformation, a metamorphosis of consciousness in all sentient beings, we must begin to experience in a profound and authentic way our absolute oneness with all life on the planet. As my hand is a part of me, nonseparate, dependent upon the body to which it is attached, so I am a part of the world—inseparable, attached, inter-dependent with it. Reaching this awareness is inextricably tied to the experience of personal trans-formation. Global transformation can only occur simultaneously with individual change.

Music is an excellent tool to use as we undergo the journey of evolutionary change. Music connects us with our essence which is movement and vibration. As we listen or play, we feel the flow, the move-ment within and around us, the utter transitoriness of life. When we are stuck in a pattern—a life situation or inner blockage which we are unwilling or unable to let go—music can open our hearts to surrender to change. As change occurs, as our hearts are opened, music comforts and makes exquisite the pain we feel. It releases us from the mind's tenacious, fearful grasp and gives an assurance of safety in the midst of uncertainty.

As we proceed on the journey of transformation, we may use music at every stage, helping us to move, flow, open, surrender.

Exercise: Musician and Transformation

The two parts of this exercise are closely related. It is helpful to have someone to change the recording for you after the first section. It is also desirable to have a friend act as a silent witness to your ritual act of transformation.

1. Choose a recording of music that you find particularly inspiring, reverent, and peaceful. Lie on

the floor in a relaxed manner, eyes closed. Breathe gently, observing the rise and fall of the abdomen as you inhale and exhale for a few moments as the music begins.

Visualize the people and the things of this life that are most precious to you. Feel their presence and their significance in your life. Allow the music to begin moving them slowly and gently away from you, leaving you alone. Feel your own life as you now know it fall away. Imagine yourself floating in empty space, no longer bound by physical or emotional ties to this world. Let the music float with you, suspend you in this realm of no-thingness. As the music ends, rest in the silence and emptiness.

2. A second piece of music should be energizing, vital, life-enhancing. Lie on the floor in a fetal or curling leaf position, eyes closed. Observe your breath as your body becomes softer, quieter. Imagine you are a seed in the earth. Feel the music moving through the soil like water, nourishing you, helping you grow. Let the music begin moving you; feel yourself flowing toward the sunlight, toward birth. Moving as slowly as you wish, gradually rise into a standing position, a flower in the sunlight unfolding more and more, a new being.

Musician as Healer

We are complete, perfect, whole, holographic—
miniature universes. Within the microcosm that is the
individual, the myriad elements are evolving toward a
consciousness of wholeness. We are organic spheres
of unity composed of physical, emotional, mental,
and spiritual fields, all interconnecting and inter-
dependent upon one another.

We may define health as an awareness of our
individual wholeness and of our existence as part of
the greater whole. Illness or disease is ignorance
of our totality, an illusion of separateness, the isolation of any aspect of our being from the whole. When a
part of the body feels somehow out of harmony
with the whole, tension arises and disease moves in as
the estranged part attempts to "take over." As we
become more aware of our inherent perfection, our
wholeness, we become healthier, no longer prone to
disharmony, imbalance, disease. To the extent that we
acknowledge our totality, we are healthy, whole, holy.

Because we are one with ourselves and with each
other, we are capable, perhaps in reality designed, to
bring about the awareness of wholeness in each
other. We are all healers. As our vision of health is

seen as the integration and synthesis of all aspects of our being, as we recognize our innate capabilities as healers of self and others, we begin to heal wisely and well.

Each of us may heal through the insightful application of our unique personality and skills. Due to the enormous advances in medical technology, members of the medical profession with their educated skills have been given almost total responsibility for our health. Many people have willingly abdicated their own inner healers in favor of the so-called experts. In reality, we are our own experts. We heal ourselves, just as we make ourselves sick. There is always a doctor in the house, if we will but acknowledge the healer within. Taking responsibility for our own health is the beginning of wholeness.

Healers are centered, rooted in their own inner beingness. They move outward from that center with sensitivity and caring. A mark of willingness to feel and express unconditional love is their detachment from results. They are effective in healing in direct proportion to their own degree of wholeness. This truth becomes glaringly obvious in the field of mental health and in the care of the dying, where we are brought face to face with our own demons and with the prospect of our own mortality. To attempt to work as a healer in these fields without seeing our own need for wholeness is ultimately counterproductive. As we acknowledge our own search for perfect health, we open to our personal healing while we are working to heal others.

Musicians are in a unique position to act as healers. Their tool, music, is enormously practical in bringing about integration. There is a strong likelihood that they are relatively whole, at least while performing:

they are connected with the physical body through the voice or their instruments; the music puts them in touch with feelings which are then expressed through sound in healthy, vitalizing ways; their mental faculties are involved to a substantial degree while they are playing. Because they are connected with physical, emotional, and intellectual faculties, the spirit is awake and operating throughout their whole being. They are available for healing others because of their own relatively whole state.

The greatest obstacle for musicians as healers may be lack of awareness, ignorance of their potential and that of music for healing. Many performers want to be recognized for their talent, to receive ego-gratification through demonstration of their skills. To awaken to the healing potential of the art, musicians must recognize their own need and desire for wholeness. This requires surrender of the ego so that the inner healer may emerge. More and more musicians are turning to the music of spirit, that of the inner being, dedicating their art to healing themselves and others, and ultimately the healing of the planet.

Music therapy is being used in the care of the physically and emotionally handicapped, the aged, and in hospices for the dying. It is taking a prominent role in the medical scene, where synthetic drugs and scientific technology are gradually making way for the ancient forms of healing through spirit.

There are infinite possibilities for healing through music. As musicians begin to see their own need for healing, as they see that in healing others they are coming to their own wholeness, as they discover the unlimited potential of their art as a healing agent for self and others, they will find ways appropriate to their unique personality, their own talent, in which to heal body and spirit through music.

Exercise: Musician as Healer

Choose a recording of music that is gentle, simple, flowing like a river. It may be something you played and recorded yourself when you were feeling calm and centered.

Lie on the floor with eyes closed, breathing gently and evenly. As the music begins, feel it moving into your body, softly and peacefully. You may feel its entrance at any point: your ears, the top of your head, the soles of your feet, your heart, your fingertips.

If you have been aware of an area that is tense or painful, it may help to have the sound enter from some distance away from that, so that you can experience the flow and movement of the music for a while before it reaches that area. Observe the music when it comes to a place where it seems to slow or to be obstructed altogether; let the music remain there for awhile. Feel the rhythm and hear the melody filling, permeating the blocked space. Imagine that the music is telling that area that it is part of the whole, that the music will connect it with the whole. Allow the music to remain in the obstructed place until there is an opening, a release, a surrender, a flow.

Feel the music moving slowly and peacefully through the entire body, connecting the parts and bringing them together into wholeness.

III

The Instrument

Relating to the Instrument

Vibration is the living, dynamic energy of the universe. To make this vibration audible and within the range of our physical senses, an instrument is required. The primal instrument is the voice. Before the discovery of sound-producing hollow logs or gourds or the beating of two sticks together, early peoples were no doubt groaning, sighing, humming, making a kind of music. The voice continues to be the primary musical instrument. It is within us as an integral part of the physical body, the thread connecting our inner and outer worlds. It is a channel of expression for our emotional and spiritual natures. The beginning music student in India must spend several months or even years studying voice before even picking up a musical instrument. The flute or vina or sitar is then taken up as an extension of the human voice.

The musical instrument is a living being, created for the express purpose of capturing vibrations from the inner world of sound and carrying them out into the physical realm as music. It is said that in India, the highest quality vina (stringed instrument) is made from the jackwood tree growing in groves near temples; the wood is said to absorb the beautiful sounds of the temple bells and retain those vibrations to become a rich, melodious instrument.

The musician's choice of instrument is tied ineluctably to his or her inner being. It is as though the incarnating soul chooses not only the circumstances of birth but also decides upon a life as a musician, realizing that this will bring the necessary experiences for growth and evolution. Included in this choice is the instrument that most nearly resembles, in temperament, vibration, character, the corresponding nature of the incarnating musician. At some specific time, often early in life, the budding musician sees and recognizes the instrument that will be his or her principle mode of expression and evolution throughout this lifetime.

Most musicians can recall with great clarity their first meeting with their chosen instrument: the singer discovering the lovely sounds her voice can produce; the pianist climbing up on the bench to survey that amazing panorama of black and white keys; the flautist reaching for his first wooden or bamboo or silver flute. The curiosity, the excitement and wonder of that first encounter remains with the musician throughout life.

A sacred relationship exists between the musician and the instrument, which is an extension of the player. Depending on the facility of the performer, the expression of the inner being is carried through the hollow reed or across the strings and out into the world of listeners. Musicians cannot be less than one with that which expresses their inner nature. Any feeling of separation between the player and the instrument is sensed and heard, consciously or unconsciously, by the listener. The hallmark of real artists is the clear communication, via their instruments, of the inner Self to the world. This is the expression of the musician Self through the extended Self, the instrument, to the other Self, the listener.

The instrument as an expressive and sacred extension of oneself—this is the relationship, the unity, musicians must establish so that their inner music may be heard.

Exercise: the Instrument

Sit quietly, eyes closed, with your instrument. Feel the primal relationship existing between yourself and it. Keeping your eyes closed, begin exploring the instrument with your hands, touching all its surfaces (including the legs and underside of the piano). Feel the shape and texture, the hardness or softness, the temperature. Put your nose against it and inhale its odors. You might want to taste it. Explore it as you would a new part of your body, a recently added appendage. Discover its dimensions, feel its mass and weight. Explore its cavities, its empty spaces.

With your eyes still closed, feel the materials with which the instrument is made. Recall the origins of those materials: see your instrument as it was in its original, organic state (I see my piano as an elephant and a rosewood tree).

When you feel thoroughly familiar with your instrument through touch and taste and smell and memory, open your eyes. Observe its dimensions, its shape, its size and color. Now begin playing, your new perceptions enhancing and enriching the music that pours forth.

Tuning the Instrument

To express our innermost nature through music, a finely tuned instrument is essential. The process of tuning is not only a means of preparing the instrument; we are also tuning our bodies, minds, and hearts to be at one within ourselves and with the instrument. Until this unity is achieved, we cannot expect the voice of the heart to be heard through our music.

How can we become one with an object? First we need to discover the areas of similarity between the object and ourselves. One time-honored method is to become that which we would know; that is, to discover the essence of the rose we must experience ourselves as the rose experiences itself. To begin, we look for the obvious relationships. The rose, like us, is a living being. It is born, lives, decays, dies; it takes in substance from the air and breathes out a different substance; it reproduces. Aesthetically it is beautiful, graceful, colorful, fragrant. It provides pleasure for the senses without demanding a return; we might say that it gives unconditionally. So to become one with the rose we must identify with these qualities, the essence of the flower. We have to discover within ourselves that same beauty, grace, and unconditioned beingness. As we are able to relate to the rose in this way, we are approaching oneness with that which outwardly seems different, separate, "other" than ourselves.

In the same way, we may attain oneness with our instrument. It has been designed to produce vibrations as a means of communicating with the outer world. Our bodies, too, have been created in such a way that we may communicate with the world in which we live. The instrument is changed and augmented as it is filled with vibration, as the breath, the fingers, the body come in contact with it. When the sound is produced, the essence of the instrument is altered subtly. The human beings, too, expand, change, open as they are touched and moved by and filled with the vibrations of the world.

Since the instrument is an extension of the musician, the tuning of that instrument coincides with the tuning or attunement of one's inner being. As the sound is dependent upon a correctly tuned instrument, so the music proceeding from the heart of the musician depends upon the attunement, the at-one-ment, of the inner life. An out-of-tune instrument is unavailable for the expression of beautiful sound. It will not do what the musician desires because it cannot. Similarly, the player who is out of tune within, unconnected by spirit to all aspects of his being—body, mind, feelings—cannot express the music of spirit. A perfectly tuned instrument becomes a clear channel for the expression of the most beautiful sound. The musician who is perfectly in harmony with his inner nature becomes a clear channel for the communication of spirit, the inner and outer substance that is the essence of music.

When the musician begins tuning his instrument in preparation for playing, he is at the same time connecting with his center, bringing his body, mind, and feelings into alignment and harmony with his inmost spirit. As the strings are sounded and stretched or loosened, the musician becomes aware of tension and release occurring in his body. He focuses his mind completely on the present moment. He opens to his feelings, making them available to his music and to his listeners. While the ear is the witness to the tuning of the outer musical instrument, the silent observer or spirit witnesses the alignment, the gathering together in the center all aspects of the musician. Thus the ear is connected tangibly with the inner being. The instrument comes into tune and readiness for playing as the musician moves toward wholeness of being.

Singers warm up the voice; this is their method of tuning the instrument. At the same time they are bringing the entire being to attention and readiness for performance. Some singers are unaware of the inner effects of voice warmup, but if it is done consciously, with attention and love, the ensuing music will be pervasive and powerful.

While it may be impractical or impossible for the pianist to tune her instrument, there is a period before she starts playing when she attunes herself to the piano as it is. This may require more openness, more letting go, than that needed by the guitarist, for instance, who can tune the guitar to his liking. The pianist must become one with the piano through total surrender of her own being to the instrument; the instrument tunes the musician.

All things of a material nature, despite their diversity of form, are basically composed of the same stuff: dancing electrons, a maze of energy whirling in larger energy fields. As musicians play, their own dancing atoms join with those of the instruments, and a greater movement is choreographed, emerging as rhythm, tone, pitch—music.

Aware of this cosmic ballet, we begin tuning the instrument and ourselves in a loving, joyful way, a kind of warmup at the barre before the dance begins. While we stretch the strings, shorten or lengthen the flute, tighten or loosen the head of the drum, we simultaneously balance our inner being. Breathing deeply, relaxing tension, we prepare the mind, body, and heart for the emergence of sound through that finely tuned extension of the inner being, the instrument.

Exercise: Tuning the Instrument*

Our preference for a particular musical instrument tells us much about who we are and what we wish to express, because the instrument can expand and enhance our unique, personal sound. If you could play any instrument, which would you choose? Fantasize or dream about this for a while. When you have decided, try this exercise:

Become the instrument you have chosen. Verbally describe all the aspects of the instrument as though you are describing yourself. Feel what it is like to be that instrument. For example: "I am a flute. I am a hollow tube. I am shining. When breath pours through me, beautiful sounds go forth." See how many different ways you can define the instrument, always

*Adapted from a workshop by Carolyn Kenny. Printed by permission.

107

beginning with "I." Speaking aloud can make it more real. You might tape your descriptions and refer back to them from time to time. You may want to write about this experience. Whenever you play your instrument or hear your chosen instrument being played, recall this exercise as you listen.

IV

The Space

The Shape of Space

As we gaze into the heavens on a star-studded night, we feel wonder, awe, a sense of our own insignificance in the presence of such vastness and emptiness. We marvel at the length of time, measured in human lifetimes, necessary for a trip to the nearest star, even if we could travel at the speed of light.

Of all the physical realities we live with, the concept of space may be the most intangible, the least accessible to the reasoning mind, and the most elusive to our perceptions and senses. Space is unfelt, unheard, invisible; we can perceive it only through its contents. Empty space is unimaginable. Objects describe boundaries, telling us that there is space, something which separates individual entities. Just as time may be the medium which prevents everything from happening at once, so space makes possible the perception of individualities, of separateness.

One of the startling discoveries of recent decades has been that of black holes, masses of energy so condensed that there is virtually no space, only energy. A black hole may be the embryo of a new galaxy or solar system, energy packed tightly in a womb eventually to explode outward in a powerful "Big

111

Bang." It may also represent the death place of a solar system or galaxy that has imploded upon itself, as space shrinks and finally disappears altogether.

While physicists explore the physical realities of space and nonspace, mystics view space as an illusion, the maya of existence, necessary for our world of duration and boundaries, a concept to be dropped, to see through or around. Both the physical and spiritual nature of space may be valid in a total perspective of reality. We may discover this through an exploration of our own inner nature, for the space within us is identical to and coexistent with the space surrounding us. During the practice of meditation, we can become aware of that inner space. As we center our attention on it, we feel it move, alter, expand. In the same way, we can come to feel the expansiveness of our surrounding space, our environment, as we put our attention upon it.

Space is not a container but is itself contained within our consciousness. As we become more fully awake and aware, we expand, and the space within and around us expands accordingly. This growth in spaciousness is creative, life-giving, healing. Stephen Levine, who has had extensive experience in caring for the dying, often speaks of this spaciousness. He describes the impulse to contract and fold in around our physical or emotional pain. He points out the benefits of providing space for the pain, of opening to it and expanding the space so that the pain may breathe, so to speak. Thus pain becomes less excruciating and easier to bear.

Dancers are intimately attuned to the space around them, molding it, shaping it with their movements. Space is intrinsic to sculpture and architecture. Because music is not in itself a visual art, however, there is little emphasis on the role of space in the creation of sound. Concert halls, recording studios, and musical instruments are all designed primarily for the purpose of containing and enhancing sound. The musician is often unaware of the capability of sound to shape the space in which it occurs. The molding of space through sound is an invisible and subtle process. Musicians and listeners alike are generally unconscious of the space-shaping. But when a great artist touches and moves the audience with music, magic occurs, and we have palpable evidence that the space surrounding and filling us is moving, changing, flowing with the sound. Our breath, our bodies, our emotions are creating a space within the sound as well.

Rupert Sheldrake, a respected biologist, in his book *A New Science of Life* connects the physical reality of cellular, molecular biology with the non-material realm of consciousness. In effect, he states that there is a collective unconscious of the physical world; this may be parallel to Jung's collective unconscious of the psyche. Sheldrake proposes the existence of fields outside our ordinary perceptions of time and space in which all events are recorded, a sort of genetic account for future generations to draw from, add to, or learn by. The DNA helix would be the physical manifestation of these genetic records. He calls them "morphogenetic fields." They may be related to what Eastern religions call the akashic record, a sort of all-encompassing history of consciousness.

The great nineteenth-century physicist Michael Faraday hypothesized that a person's actual boundaries are established, not by the physical body, but by the extent to which one's influence is felt. Thus a woman in California is present in some way, perhaps morphogenetically, with her lover in New York. They are in the same field of consciousness. We have all experienced feelings of the presence or nearness to someone "close" to us, regardless of separations of time or space. The scientific community may be uncovering a reality that begins to explain what distance or proximity really means.

The morphogenetic-field theory has far-reaching implications for musicians. Imagine a field, a space in which all music ever played reverberates, a field in which musicians hear not only what has been played, but into which they each pour their own music. They expand the field as they are enriched by it. As we marvel at the incredible musical abilities of more and more young musicians, we can imagine that they are living in an evolving, intelligent field of music from which they receive information and inspiration.

If we believe that every note we play becomes part of a continuing musical field, our sense of responsibility toward our art expands correspondingly. Whether we have listeners or not, the music we play is influencing the field. We have the opportunity of bringing into the field that which we want to be there. There is an eternity of sound from which we are drawing and to the evolution of which we are contributing. This concept is applicable in all fields such as business, politics, science. Since music is one of the most direct and powerful purveyors of thought, feeling, and consciousness, however, its field may be the most expansive and influential of all fields. Every life form is influenced by vibration; thus the sound field is extremely significant.

While related to physical nature, the morphogenetic fields are states of consciousness as well.

They are not localities in space, but there is a kind of space within them with the potential for expansion, evolution, transformation. A musician performing baroque music in a concert hall is dwelling in the field of all baroque music that has ever been played. The audience is also in the field, partaking of its contents and contributing dynamic attention and response—breath and heartbeat and applause. The feeling of expansion or spaciousness that emerges from the appreciative listeners influences the field. Conscious contact with the field releases tremendous energy and creativity. We can gauge the extent of our contact with the field by the feeling of opening or spaciousness that occurs within us as we listen or perform.

Exercise: The Shape of the Space

1. Sit quietly, with your instrument at hand if you have one. Look around the room; notice its contents and empty places, its dimensions. Tune your senses to the odors, temperature, humidity, the physical feel of the room.

Now close your eyes and feel the space within you. Imagine the vast distances between the protons and electrons that make up your body; feel the infinite capacity of your inner space for expansion. Imagine that your body is an empty balloon waiting to be filled with an endless stream of air.

When you can feel this expansive quality of your inner space, begin playing your instrument or singing. Allow the music to stretch your inner space, to extend it until it meets the outer space surrounding you. Feel the boundaries between inner and outer fade and dissolve. Visualize the sound moving, altering, shaping, transforming the space. Continue playing in that field of no-boundaries where inner and outer space have become one.

When you have finished playing, you may want to draw or paint or sculpt a visual image of the form the space has taken through playing your music. You might experiment with different musical modes— your own improvisations, jazz, classical music— observing the differences in your perceptions of space as shaped through various types of music.

2. Play or listen to a piece of music from a certain era by a particular composer. If possible, place a picture of the composer nearby. Begin playing the piece or listening to a recording of it, feeling the presence of the composer as well as all the people who have ever performed it. Immerse yourself in that composer's field. Acknowledge the gifts you are receiving from the field and your own contribution to it as you play or listen.

3. Generally, we think of our bodies as the yang principle, the initiator, moving through space which is yin, the receiver. For now, visualize space as yang, the animator, penetrating your body which is yin, the receptacle.

Choose a recording of music you enjoy moving or dancing to. As the music begins, stand with eyes closed, breathing gently, in a relaxed position. Feel the sound moving through, permeating, defining the space that surrounds you.

When you are ready, begin moving with the sound. Open yourself completely to receive the music. Feel the yin-ness of your body mingling and joining with the yang-ness of space. Allow the space, the music, to penetrate and fill and vitalize your body, bringing you to an awareness and acceptance of your wholeness, your inner balance of yin and yang.

When the music ends, wait in the silence, allowing that sense of integration to remain with you. Carry it into every space you enter.

4. Practice walking, running, speaking, singing as though you are the receiver rather than the giver, that which is moved rather than that which initiates. Allow everyone and everything in your environment to enter and fill and transform you. This requires an attitude of gentleness, openness, surrender.

V
The Listener

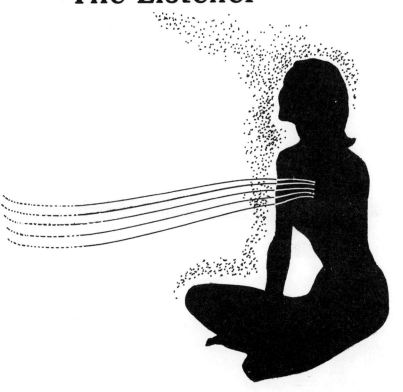

Uniting with the Listener

There is always a listener when music is played. The musician listens as well as plays. In performance, as listener the musician is one with the "other"—the listening audience. It is this other, the audience, the receiver of the sound, with whom the musician must ultimately be concerned. For many performers this concern remains at the ego level: the musician desires recognition, response, acclaim. Many musicians readily admit that is their goal. If they remain at this level, their music eventually stagnates; artistry cannot emerge.

To move beyond the realm of ego in the smallest way marks an important shift for the performer. This may occur as the musician places total emphasis on the quality of the music, listener be damned. Or it may be a turning inward, a changed view point—more concern for artistry, less need for adulation of others. This is a necessary phase in the performer's career.

In the nonperforming arts such as painting, sculpting, or writing, artists may remain comfortably with their focus on artistry since they do not usually deal directly with their audience. It is a one-directional communication, a monologue. They cannot feel the response of the audience because they lack physical proximity. Performers, on the contrary, are continually dealing with the audience and their relationship to it. If they ignore the listeners, they close themselves to a valuable and necessary creative source: the receiver of the music.

True artists understand and respect the importance of the role of the audience. They acknowledge the listener, the other, as that missing part of the music and of their being. They receive not only information, energy, and inspiration; the audience provides the cup into which their music flows. This cup, this receptacle, is essential to the sound. The audience is the feminine, receiving aspect of musical performance.

While the listener completes the performance and is its final goal, the major responsibility for communication lies with the performer. If musicians are attuned to the listeners, if through awareness of their duality with the audience they can attain unity with them, true artistry will emerge. The genuine artist knows what is needed and is willing to allow it to happen.

The audience, on the other hand, is often ignorant of any obligation to the artist. We go to a performance to be entertained, moved, uplifted, or to be seen in our new clothes. We pay our money, sit back comfortably, and wait for magic to transpire. In bars and restaurants, the musician seems simply to be supplying background music for eating, drinking, socializing. Even when we attend a concert with the express purpose of hearing music, we are seldom aware of our responsibility as the receiving half of the musical experience. Since the advent of recorded music and television, we have become passive observers rather than active participants in the audience mode.

An exception to this may be found in India, where audiences seem to realize that listening can be a meditation, a dynamic response which enhances the performance and performer as well as the listener's own enjoyment. Indians also believe that applause provides physical energy for the musician, an important contribution to the performance. Western audiences are beginning to appreciate Indian music, not only through an increasing familiarity with it, but also because the music and performers draw the listeners subtly but compellingly into active, participatory listening.

Active listening requires attention, stillness, openness, spaciousness. As performers are in contact with inner silence and spaciousness, and as they express these qualities through the music, the audience responds accordingly. Thus a two-way communication and exchange of energy becomes possible, in which music carries messages from the heart of the performer to the listener and back again.

Exercise: Uniting with the Listener

The next time you are planning to attend a musical performance, prepare yourself in the following way:

Sit quietly, eyes closed, breath gentle and even. Allow thoughts of anticipation about the coming performance to flow through you. As visions of the performer, the composer, the anticipated sound come to you, let them enter and permeate you. As they become part of your inner being, feel yourself uniting with the artists, the music, the rest of the audience, until all is blended into a whole. When you arrive for the performance, carry the feelings of wholeness with you. As the music begins, close your eyes and move back into that remembered space.

The Listening Mind

The art of listening has been neglected for a very long time, perhaps since the invention of the printing press made the words of the storyteller available to the eye as well as to the ear. In the evolution of technology, certain capabilities of the mind have been developed and emphasized while other aspects have been disparaged or forgotten. While reading involves abstraction—a moving away from the actual—listening to nonverbal sounds such as a mantra or music is a direct experience of reality.

It is difficult to decide which of these modes of perception is more valuable. We do need to understand the ways in which our ability to read, to translate symbols into an image of reality, has shaped and altered our listening faculties. When a new skill is learned, there is the temptation to apply it in as many situations as possible. So when we learn to read, when we discover that we can translate abstract symbols into some kind of meaning, we begin applying this skill to our senses of sight, touch, taste, smell, hearing. Our finely honed minds move beyond the primal message of the senses. Something tastes not salty but "too" salty, therefore not "good." We touch the bark of a tree and determine not only that it is, indeed, bark, but that it is rough and thus unpleasant to the touch. We move a step away from the direct experience of the senses through the mind's two-edged sword of discrimination and judgment.

Through force of habit, cultural conditioning, social pressure, personal needs and desires, the mind is engaged while listening to music. Western music in particular seems to signify order, form, structure, all defined, arranged, and conducted by the mind. Other elements of the mind are often involved as the listener hears and responds to music. During a live performance, we are impressed in one way or another by the reputation of the musicians; by all the music we've ever heard, especially in the mode we are hearing; by the space in which the music is heard; by the other members of the audience; by the dress, gender, and general appearance of the performers; and by the ways in which the music itself fits in with our preconceived ideas of how it should or should not sound. If all or most of the elements of the performance are what we would describe as favorable, our pleasure will be great. If something's off, a too-formal attire of the performer, a restless audience, or an uncomfortable chair, our enjoyment level may descend until we wonder why we bothered to come. These may seem formidable barriers to the profound experience of unconditional listening.

The most satisfying musical experience for the mind-engaged listener may be the jazz performance. Though jazz is often performed in nightclubs filled with smoke, clattering glassware, and noisy customers, the dedicated fan tunes all that out through utter concentration on the music. Jazz can be intellectually gratifying with its improvisations based on orderly progressions of chords. The more familiar the piece, the more enjoyable it is to listen to the musician's creativity moving through the familiar territory of the harmonic structure. The mind can be undistracted as it focuses on the music.

This is true of classical music as well. Anticipation, climax, tension, release provide the mind with food for thought. But the mind's reliance on familiarity, on order and structure, can be a very real obstacle to the act of hearing and receiving the sound as it is. Familiarity and anticipation take us away from the present moment. Allowing the sound to simply pour into our ears without judgment or prejudice, making no demands, but receiving the pulse, the tonality or atonality as it is—this is the listening skill that many of us have neglected or cast aside as primitive and uncultured, hence useless.

There is a story about an intellectual who wanted to know more about Zen, so he went to a Zen master. The master began pouring tea into the visitor's cup. The tea spilled over the brim of the cup, but the master continued to pour. The intellectual said, "My cup is full; it will hold no more." The Zen master replied, "Yes. And like your cup, your mind is filled with your own precious ideas. You must first empty the cup before I can give you anything."

To come to a performance with an empty cup and no expectation other than that something will occur, to listen with a still, empty mind, to experience on the primary sensual level the performers and the music—all this is necessary for a profound listening experience. In the so-called empty mind is an awareness of all that is happening in the sound, in the field in which it occurs, and within the listener. This awareness comes as the contents of the mind are let go.

Exercise: the Listening Mind

Plan to attend a musical performance of a kind you have never been to, for whatever reason. Perhaps you dislike or are unfamiliar with that type of music; you think you are too old or too young for it; it is not your kind of music or performer.

Just before attending, sit quietly with eyes closed, breathing evenly and gently. As you inhale, feel your breath as a cool autumn breeze moving into your head. Feel it swirling around, reaching every part of your brain, sweeping it clean of its contents. As you exhale, feel all the debris moving out of your body, leaving behind an empty room, clean and fresh.

If you can, repeat the exercise as you sit in the hall waiting for the performance to begin. See if you can listen to the entire performance with that freshness.

The Listening Body

When we speak of art in any form, we know at once that the physical body is involved, for art connects the body and matter with the soul or spirit. The practice of art engages mental, emotional, and spiritual qualities. The body is involved in all these. It is the vessel or container as well as the means of expression for all aspects of the psyche in the material world.

Hearing is a physical phenomenon performed by a remarkable sensory organ, the ear. Our ears are small apertures, opening to larger chambers inside the head. When we listen, we are opening to more spaciousness, to greater knowledge and growth and awareness. This expansion is echoed throughout the body; it is as though we are breathing through our ears and consciousness is being carried into our cells like oxygen, stretching and feeding them.

The art of listening requires stillness. While we seem to be an inherently social, voluble, speech-oriented species, our deeper essence is silence: the matrix from which sound and speech emerge. As we sit in meditation, allowing ourselves to become conscious of the inner being, a growing silence is palpable evidence that we are approaching the Self.

In this silence we might feel and hear the continuous activity of the body: the flow of blood, the beat of the heart proceeding out of the silence. During meditation these bodily processes may slow, but only in rare cases, such as those of yogis in samadhi, do they appear to halt.

The physical body can be the most powerful distraction for our awareness of silence. A headache, an upset stomach, irregularity of the bowels demand our immediate attention. Putting the mind on other things may be difficult or impossible. Pleasure as well as pain draws our attention directly to its source. Our awareness can be dependent upon the whims of the body unless we are adepts at forgetting or moving out of the body in one way or another. Attempts to leave the body may be an easy way out of having to deal with the material world, a sort of denial of the physicality of our existence. But if matter and spirit are one, if the body is one with the Self, it is then unrealistic, in the most profound sense of the word, to deny it as an integral part of our reality.

A solution to the problem of distraction may be to use the body as a means of focusing attention. To place the attention on a physical sensation such as an itch, to allow its full expression, somehow helps to diffuse or dissolve that sensation, freeing our awareness for whatever else is at hand. Until we attend to what is happening at the physical level, sensation can continue to distract us. Our senses are messengers; they continue to prod us until we notice them and heed their reports. When we can look upon any so-called distraction as a communication, hence a focus for our attention, it dissipates or dissolves or else persists and tells us what we need to know. When this is recognized, we are freed from distraction.

129

We can then focus our attention wherever we choose. The art of listening requires this freedom.

When we achieve an inner stillness, it is as though the body is swimming in a sea of silence. Immersing ourselves in this sea, we may feel the Self as an inner rhythmic flow, continuous and palpable—the movement within the stillness, the silence within the sound. The ideal meditation may be in contacting that silence as we go about the physical activities of eating, walking, talking, or playing music.

Exercise: The Listening Body

1. Put on a favorite piece of music. Sit or stand quietly, eyes closed, breathing slowly and gently. Become aware of the music entering your consciousness through your ears. Feel the sound pouring through those tiny openings at the sides of your head and flowing into your body.

Now stretch your arms toward the source of music, palms facing out. Allow the sound to enter your body through the palms of your hands. Observe without judgment any physical sensations that may arise as your hands receive the sound.

Lie on the floor with the soles of your feet near the speaker. Feel the music moving into you through your feet. Try using different parts of your body as "ears" for the sound.

Finally, open your eyes and gaze softly at the source of the sound. Allow the music to enter your body through your eyes, observing what happens to your gaze as you feel the music entering there.

When the music ends, remain in the silence, feeling your whole body as a receiving instrument that has received and now contains the music.

2. Put on a piece of orchestral or choral music. Become the musical conductor, directing the sound. Feel full responsibility for the music. Use free, energetic movements in your conducting.

Now play the piece again, but this time let the music inform your movements. Allow the sound to tell your body what to do, how to move. With the mind still and not interfering, feel the music conducting your body. Give the sound full responsibility for your movements.

The Listening Heart

While hearing is an action of the body and the mind, true listening begins within the heart. Speech occurs through the processes of intellect, but real communication, communion, can take place only in the hearts of the speaker and the listener. When we listen without actually hearing, without taking in and becoming one with that which is heard, we are not listening with the heart.

There is a point in the chest midway between the nipples which someone has named the "grief center." When we apply even slight pressure to this spot, we find it is extremely tender, and there is usually pain when it is pressed. This is the heart center, the region within that contains our grief, our suffering, our sorrow. Underlying the sorrow, however, is joy, spirit, Self.

To reach the Self we must open to and move through the pain harbored in the heart. Because modern society is obsessed with avoiding, masking, or refusing to acknowledge pain at all costs, our hearts are often closed tightly like a fist. We do not want to feel pain, and consequently we feel very little of anything. We shut out joy in our fear of hurt. That fist within the chest becomes more and more constricted, a shell forms around it as "hard-heartedness" sets in, and we close ourselves off from connectedness, from communication, from love.

As we so carefully block the world from entering the inner sanctum, we also prevent the love within, our essence, from flowing outward. This lack of flow from within can be far more serious than just shutting out the world. The repressed energy of the heart center then finds other modes of release: anger, emotional or physical disease, ultimately perhaps a heart attack, perhaps for some the heart's loudest, most agonizing plea for release, for opening, for freedom.

Opening the heart, becoming receptive and willing to allow the flow of feeling in and out, may be the most effective spiritual practice we can undertake. For when the heart is open wide, vulnerable, and breathing freely, we invite all of life to enter in, and we also allow all that is within to flow outward to the world. In this state of openness, of movement and flow, the heart is fully engaged in listening.

For some individuals the heart never closed; they have remained in a state of receptivity and vulnerability like that of the very young. For most of us, however, life has dealt blows that made closing the heart the only means of survival. Yet there are many ways to open the heart. The miraculous process of conceiving and giving birth to a child can be an effective heart-opener for a woman. As the father becomes more of an active participant in the birthing process, he also has access to the kind of heart-opening that women enjoy as their biological right.

The care of another living being, whether plant, animal or human, is a way to the heart. Religion, meditation, prayer are other pathways to the door of the heart. The opening of that door seems to require a dynamic force: serving others, creating or performing art, involving oneself in the world with selflessness and love.

Often the heart is torn open through passion, grief, or terror. The death of a loved one, the onset of a catastrophic illness, a dramatic change in life style—any of these may blast directly into the heart, ripping it open (for that is how it feels), and leaving it raw, unprotected, vulnerable. If we can practice opening our hearts consciously bit by bit, a terrorist attack at the gates may not be necessary.

A wonderful aspect of the open heart is its willingness to take in sorrow or grief with love and compassion. The openness provides space for our pain to unfold, to be, and perhaps eventually to dissolve. As we open to our pain and embrace it, giving it breathing space, our hearts are enlarged to take in more, even the pain of the whole world. From this, compassion is born. Stephen Levine defines compassion as the meeting of another's pain with love. Until we are willing to receive whatever the world may offer, our hearts will be little more than muscular pumps that sustain physical life.

Music carries us directly to the heart. Everyone has experienced that immediate sense of opening when a certain piece of music is heard. The sound moves through all resistance, passing directly into the heart, making itself at home there, an intruder where all else is unwelcome. This power of music to penetrate our most carefully barricaded spaces has been acknowledged since the beginning of time. It is as if the heart is the true home of music; the sound moves there naturally and remains. The process of opening the heart is considerably enhanced through the use of music.

When a person is grieving but unwilling or unable to feel that grief fully, music can bring out the pain. Many of us have learned to avoid listening to certain music at times of sorrow, wanting to avoid the hurt. Sometimes we cling to our grief, using it as an affirmation of our love, so we listen to music that will hold us in that place. We are often unskilled in the conscious use of music to open our hearts to joy. Deliberately choosing and listening to certain kinds of music can lead to a natural kind of opening that occurs without our conscious participation.

Designers of background music that is played in offices and stores and elevators have carefully researched the effects of music on the emotions and the physical body. They have learned what sounds will energize or relax listeners. They do not, however, aim at the heart, because they know that the music must not engage the innermost being: work might stop; we might decide to go fishing or write a poem or hug our fellow workers. Because of its built-in innocuousness, background music cannot reach the heart. While we may feel we can successfully block it out, its subliminal effects still influence us to some degree.

Listening to music is identical with involvement in any art. One's whole being must be engaged. The heart connection affects body and mind and encompasses the whole person. The music we love is that which makes this heart connection possible. True communication with others begins with the touching and opening of our own hearts. Music brings us to that communion with simplicity and immediacy.

Exercise: The Listening Heart

Choose a recording of music that is particularly

moving for you. As it plays, sit quietly, breathing gently and evenly. Focus your attention on the heart center, the point midway between the nipples. Allow the music to enter that place. Imagine the sound flowing through an opening, however small, into the inner chambers of your heart (not your physical heart but a center of energy called a *chakra* in yoga philosophy). Feel the music as water or a sweet fragrance swirling around in your heart. Observe any expansion, any opening or spaciousness that seems to be occurring. Use your mind simply to observe, not to manipulate; let the music do the opening.

As you feel your heart expand, become aware of the feelings that reside there. Feel the music opening, making room, giving breathing space to those feelings, whatever they might be.

When the music ends, remain in the silence that keeps the heart open and spacious. Carry that spaciousness with you.

For one full day, as often as possible, remind yourself to "keep the heart open." In every space between thoughts when your mind is not occupied, repeat this mantra. At the end of the day, while listening to music, allow the heart further opening and expansion.

The Listening Spirit

Listening engages the physical body through the sensory organs, the mind through attention, and the heart through compassion. But the act of listening is consummated through the gathering and integrative capacities of the spirit, the Self. This inner listener encompasses all aspects of our material, mental, and emotional selves and joins them in a sphere of organic wholeness, of oneness. While spirit permeates and enlivens every aspect of our being, it is more than the sum of our parts; it is the total environment, the whole. It orchestrates the body's utilization of the energy necessary for functioning as a material being; it directs the clear attention of the unconditioned mind; it informs the pure compassion of the open heart. Beyond this, it powers the vital force that draws sound inward and enables the outward breath, the response, to come forth.

The role of spirit as gatherer and integrator becomes obvious in the art of listening, which is dynamic action as well as passive reception. The qualities of yin and yang, receptivity and thrust, are engaged in a dance of polarities. The spirit brings about a balance of these opposites, directing us in natural, harmonious ways of participatory listening. Spirit as choreographer and conductor provides balance and space in which to carry on the dance. The circle dances of many indigenous peoples reflect this. They are graceful examples of receiving and responding, breathing out and breathing in, motion and stillness, all performed within the encompassing movement of the whole.

The spirit is observer: detached, unbiased, indifferent to results. This is a divine indifference that encompasses, not excludes, compassion, tenderness, response to what is heard simply as it is—unjudged, actual, in the present moment. In this way, spirit hears truth and is energized and enlarged through the hearing. It is nourished and transformed by sound. As we require the involvement of spirit in our listening, so does spirit need sound to fulfill its purpose. As we are aware of the needs of the spirit, even in its seeming omnipotence, we become cocreators of life and beauty.

We may use conscious will and purpose to improve our listening skills by engaging the body and mind and heart with awareness. The involvement of spirit, however, seems to come about almost by chance. Perhaps this is the meaning of grace. We have the power to create much of our lives, but there is a point at which grace or spirit manifests, bringing us new life and transformative energy for our creative endeavors. We begin then to experience serendipity, those unexpected, un-asked-for pleasures that pop out of nowhere: the gift of wind upon sails in a calm sea; the pool of clear fresh water that suddenly appears on a hot dusty trail; warm sun breaking through the clouds on a cold December afternoon. This joyful state tells us that spirit is present and awake within us.

As we listen to music, through careful observation we can discover what in us is hearing, what is involved: mind, body, heart. When spirit is fully present, we are brought in each moment to a wholly new listening experience, far beyond our ordinary perceptions and enjoyment and involvement. These are the truly magical moments when we become one with the sound; we are the sound as we are the hearer.

To discover the music that fully engages mind, heart, body, and spirit is to find a source from which we may draw at any time. This music is precious, to be cherished and honored, for it is the breath of the spirit, that vital force which is the essence of our being.

Exercise: The Listening Spirit

After attending a musical event (your own or someone else's performance) that seemed magical and transformative, find a quiet, secluded place to sit in silence. With eyes closed, breathing gently, recall the performance. Feel the music within you, how it has permeated your entire intellectual, physical, and emotional self. Observe the vitality of your body, the stillness of your mind, the openness of your heart. Feel the spaciousness, the energy, the love that the music has given you. Acknowledge and give thanks to spirit for this refreshment, this nourishment. Later, express your gratitude through your own poetry, movement, music, or art.

VI

The Communication

The Message of the Heart

Music has been called the universal language. We can communicate nonverbally through music with others who do not speak in our tongue. But it is important to realize that when we describe music as a language, we place the same limitations on it that are inherent in verbal communication. The ability to convey meaning through speech is a remarkable evolutionary skill, but we often overestimate the usefulness of this faculty. As we begin attempting to communicate with creatures of other species, for example trying to teach dolphins our language while searching for theirs, we overlook the obvious truth that we are often sadly ineffective in communicating with our own species, even when we employ a common, familiar language.

Words define, describe, convey ideas and images. At the same time they exclude, limit, ignore, or leave out that which is not spoken. Words are partial descriptions, reflecting the individual speaker's view of reality. They may be inaccurate, misleading, dishonest, even when spoken by those who have a perfect understanding and command of their language. Words are products of the mind; they are abstractions, symbols. They cannot bring about an experience of what they symbolize in any but a vicarious way. The bane of our modern society may be our heavy reliance on words to the exclusion of other means of communication.

Body language has become a popular area of study for psychologists, therapists, and counselors who are discovering that our bodily reactions may convey more accurate descriptions of our real condition than words can. We are learning that the muscles, the tissues, the cells of the body are storehouses for memories, thoughts, and feelings. Our state of health is often determined by the kinds of experiences we have stored in our bodies and by our ability to release them. Feelings of grief, anger, and fear are often denied verbal expression; instead we bury them, and their presence and energy are indicated through symptoms of tension, disharmony, dis-ease. To contact this energy, words and speech are often inadequate. Through the use of bodywork, movement, music, and other arts, we can delve into the body and begin to release the energy imprisoned there. The study of body language is a method of tapping into a deep source of knowledge for which words prove inadequate.

So music as a means of communication is more than a language. As a language it is limited by the listener's ability to be open and receptive to sound, to be nonjudgmental and unbiased and, in a way, mindless. Music is more a language of the heart, of spirit, than of mind, which is the center of speech. When we use music as a means of intellectual communication, we limit its effect because we have fixed ideas about what the music means, about what is being said, about what one wishes to hear.

Some people feel that a truly "universal" music should be constructed, a mixture or amalgamation of music from all cultures which could speak to everyone on the planet. This suggestion is mind thinking, not heart feeling. Music speaks to our wholeness: *that* is its universality. As we begin to recognize, accept, and honor our own wholeness, we can acknowledge and appreciate the wholeness of the universal music which speaks in many dialects but with one common tongue—the language of the heart.

Music communicates on many levels: physical, intellectual, emotional. But its fullness of expression and intrinsic message move from the heart of the musician and aim at the heart of the listener. Music is what music therapist and author Carolyn Kenny calls the "mythic artery: that which not so much connects but reminds us of our connection." The message is this: I am Spirit. You are Spirit. We are one in spirit, in love. Other meanings emerge as well: We are human, we feel pain, joy, terror, beauty. Our weaknesses as well as our strengths, our humanity, bind us together as one. The music gives love and asks for love; this is the only communication necessary to spirit. The universality of this message extends beyond this planet, beyond all boundaries of space and time and separateness, into the limitlessness of eternity. Music speaks of that reality as we are experiencing it in this moment.

Life is one—connected, related, whole. It proceeds from the one Source. We may call that source energy, nature, God. We not only proceed from Source, but we coexist and are at one with it as well. We do not, cannot, live apart from it; we cannot detach ourselves or be disconnected from it. In our essence, we are that Source. The illusion of our separateness is simply that, an illusion. It is the Maya of the Hindu; the shadow play in Plato's cave; the Hell of Christianity. As perceived by our senses, the physical world looks, feels, tastes, smells, sounds as though there are separate entities. My body is apart from your body; there is space between us. In order to touch or make contact, we must move through space towards each other. Our physical connection may culminate in sexual intercourse, where for a brief moment we may experience oneness. Afterwards, our bodies move apart and separation again becomes apparent.

Zuni, the cat, sits outside my window watching a squirrel dashing about high in the branches of the oak tree. Zuni, the squirrel, the oak tree, myself are all separate expressions of the one life. The physical world draws the veil of illusion before our unity. We may spend our entire lifetime behind this veil, certain that we are separate, individual, unconnected beings. Our yearning for oneness is hidden from our consciousness by our inability to see beyond physical appearances to the deeper reality of spirit. The ego, that sense of individuality in a world filled with other individuals, clings to its illusions as its only safety, its only means of survival. Our hearts, closed to the possibility of deep relatedness because of pain or loss, are blocked as well from the flow that would connect. Only the spirit within, the Self, knows of our inherent unity with all of life.

Somewhere within each of us is a homesickness, a longing for God, for love, for meaning. We all need to know, to recall, to function in our oneness. The newborn infant, separated physically from its mother, brings into this world the consciousness of its inseparability from it. Gradually, as the sense perceptions develop and the ego begins its growth, a sense of separateness also develops, and at an early age the child begins to lose awareness of its unity with life. This may be a necessary step in the evolution of our consciousness. The plight of the so-called autistic children may be their inability to respond as separate beings. Some enlightened therapists are now trying to find ways to enter the world of these children, rather than asking for their participation in ours. The autistic child may teach us a great deal about the unity of all life.

When we begin to acknowledge the illusory quality of our separate realities, we move toward an awareness of life's oneness. When we see something as an illusion, we feel the desire to lift the veil and discover how things really are. The human being may be the only life form in the evolutionary scale that feels separate, and therefore moved to work through that illusion to the reality beyond. This is conscious evolution, and the ego makes it possible and necessary.

As the illusion of separateness dissolves, awareness of our connection and interdependence with our Mother Earth is growing. We are beginning to listen to older cultures: the aborigines, the Native Americans, the native tribes of the world. The scientific technology that gave birth to nuclear physics has brought to our startled attention the irrefutable truth that in nuclear war we would all die. Nuclear technology tells us in the clearest possible way that we are one people, one planet, one life. The bomb has been called by some our greatest spiritual teacher.

As we grow in awareness of our relatedness, the responsibility to self becomes responsibility to others. We begin to see that everything we do or think or feel affects all life on the planet. We begin to realize that the love we bestow upon ourselves is felt and welcomed by all of life. There is no such fantasy as "doing one's own thing"; we are doing everyone's thing, like it or not. When we acknowledge our connections, we see that we cannot give anything—love or hate or joy or pain—to others without giving it to ourselves at the same time. Our karma, the fruit of our labors, is present in all our actions as we do unto ourselves what we are doing unto others.

A necessary step in the increasing awareness of our oneness with Source is the realization that we *are* that Source, that God is within as without, that we are part of the creative energy of the cosmos. Jesus said, "The kingdom of God is within you." The Hindu says, "Tat Twam Asi"—thou art That. We end our prayers with "Amen"—I am. I am That. This is the God within, the Source, the power by which we are created and by which we create.

As we begin to experience the love and energy of the One within, we view our lives in a broader and deeper context. Life becomes our own creation, precious, mystical, to be revered in all its myriad forms. The discovery of the God within happens simultaneously with the process of seeing God in others. Sometimes we cannot believe in our own Godhood, so we search for it in teachers, gurus, lovers, friends. Eventually we learn that these others are simply purer reflections of our own unseen divinity. With this knowledge, we see that every encounter or meeting, whether casual or intimate, sets up a holy relationship. The Jewish greeting "Shalom" means "The God in me greets the God in you." As we see that every moment is an eternal one, we realize that every person, every event, every form present in that moment is meeting in a holy place. Wherever we walk is sacred ground; whomever we meet is God.

Mystics have been describing this kind of consciousness for centuries. It is not mysterious, but natural and divine.

When we meet each other as God meeting God, there are no real differences between us. There is no hierarchy of greater or lesser intelligence, richer or poorer, aware or unaware. We encounter those who are our equals. Thus there are no teachers and students; there is only the interchange of knowledge. There are no healers and no sick; there is just the process of healing needed by patient and healer alike. There are no performers and listeners; there is simply music linking the divinity of the musician with that of the hearer.

This realization of equality is a death blow to the egoic mind, which not only separates but also judges what is better or worse, higher or lower, good or evil. Finding God within oneself and all others is a process of destroying the ego. It is giving the individual the freedom to see his oneness with the whole, dissolving the boundaries of separateness, expanding into the All. At first this may seem difficult or impossible or undesirable, but it comes about gradually as we learn to surrender and trust in the inner spiritual life as the primal Source from which all emerges.

As healers are aware of the presence of God within, they will acknowledge the one who seeks healing as another expression of God. They know that they, as healers, are not fully in touch with their own wholeness; the patient brings to them a greater awareness of their holy state, which they also do for the patient. Thus a sacred relationship is established as creator meets creator, each of them bringing the other into an expanded awareness of the inner Godhood. Lasting healing, that which brings about irreversible awareness of wholeness, occurs only through this reciprocal giving and receiving between two patients, one called healer and one called patient. The same may be said for teaching: the learning flows between two pupils, one called teacher, one called student.

The abolition of hierarchy in relationship may be one of the final steps in our evolution toward God consciousness. As we see the One in ourselves and all others, as we see our students as our teachers and our patients as our healers, we may be functioning at one of the highest levels of awareness.

The relationship between the performer and the listener began long before their first meeting in the performance hall. Both musician and listener have been preparing themselves for the encounter from the time of birth, perhaps from previous lifetimes. Musicians spend years in study, practice, honing musical skills, all the while evolving as human beings, as creations of divine consciousness. They are contacting their inner guide, the inner Voice, and becoming familiar with their own divinity as preparation for communicating that divinity to others. They learn to contact the spirit within the other in a sacred, holy communion. The more aware musicians are of this goal of their music, the more swiftly will they encounter the true listener, the one who will hear.

Listeners are no less involved in preparation for this first meeting. Years of exposure to music, of self-examination and growth resulting in more and more awareness of the inner Self have fostered a yearning for communication with the musician. They may have been seeking the music and the performer who could speak to their deepest being. There may have been times when there was a spark of recognition, when a performer spoke briefly to this inner seeking. But the need for a whole, holy relationship in which one is the receiver of the sound, the responder to the music, moves them on a continued search for communication of soul to soul through music.

At some time, the correct time, the listener finds that place with the performer in which all the ingredients for divine communication are present: two individuals, each in touch with his or her own center, yearning to make contact, become one with the center of another through the mystical flow of music between them.

The space in which this occurs is a dynamic, unified field—fluid, conscious, receptive to the energy of the persons within it. It expands as the consciousness of those entering flows through it; it becomes attentive to the sounds that will mold and shape it as the musical conversation between performer and listener commences. The space itself is listening, hearing, receiving, vibrating rhythm and tone. There is nurturing safety in this space, freedom to open up to new possibilities. It is a sacred space where holy relationship begins.

The performer is aware of his own being, the being of the listener, the being of the space. As he enters the field, he observes with clear, nonjudging mindfulness the space and its contents. He notices the physical qualities—the size, shape, temperature, colors, sounds—of the space. He looks at those who will be partaking of the music and sees them not only as physical bodies but as thinking, feeling, spiritual entities as well. He views them with loving concern, recognizing that they will fulfill the purpose of the music: ears to hear, hearts to feel, souls with which to communicate.

The musician must bring to the performance the utter confidence in the ability of spirit to reach out to spirit. This faith may be the most important quality the musician can contribute to the performance. Without it, even the most technically adroit will fail to fulfill the role of music as divine communicator. The ego, that self hoping for acclaim, must be relinquished at this time. While it has been a motivating force in propelling one toward certain musical goals, at the moment of performance the ego must be set aside so that spirit may be heard. The music, the listener, the space require this.

The musician who wants to evoke particular responses from the audience will run into difficulties. Expectations, attachment to results, desire to control or manipulate the listener through the music will invite frustration. Ram Dass says that as soon as you think you're entertaining someone, you have made the audience an object, a "them" out there; you stop the flow. Stephen Levine says that if we think we are helping someone, that is, molding that person into what we think is correct or helpful or healthy, that person is in trouble, and so are we. Many musicians see their calling as that of an entertainer who can touch their listeners in particular ways. This is an ego-desire, not a call of the spirit. It is a need for control rather than a willingness to surrender and let go. When relationship is polarized into control and submission, there is no communication, only separation, alienation, loss of contact.

To greet the other as oneself; to see the wholeness of another as one's own wholeness; to find the reality shared with the other—these are the perceptions necessary for true communication. A one-sided conversation may be fine for musicians who play for their own pleasure, but even then there is the other, the inner Self who is listening. In a performance setting, there can be no monologues. Every note, every breath, each moment sends messages between musician and listener. To ignore this two-way flow of feeling and meaning is to relinquish artistry for ego-gratification.

Risk is a crucial element in communication through music. Just as truly creative musicians must be willing to be open, to examine their inner life, to throw aside familiar comforts and plunge into the unknown, so they must take risks during performance. Opening up to oneself may be easy or difficult, depending on what is being uncovered, how long that door has remained closed and with what defenses, and the degree of centeredness with which one can confront and explore the unknown. If there is fear or discomfort, the way may be closed off and the boundary remain firmly in place until one feels more equipped to explore it. In performance, there can be no such refusal or retreat.

If there is to be communication with the listener, the musician's doors leading inward must stay open. Through this opening, the listener is invited into the reality of the musician. This involves risk for the performer and the listener as well. The inner world of the musician, the creative fount, is personal and sacred. For the nonperforming artist, the intrusion of the outside world is secondary; artists need not be physically present as their work is experienced by others. Although they have willingly opened their doors, they can choose not to be at home when others move into their reality. Communication may be unbalanced; responses are received more often through the critics than from individuals simply partaking of the art. Some artists find this frustrating. A sculptor who is a friend said to me, "You receive immediate response to your music. The only way I could really know what my audience feels would be to sit around the gallery all day, introducing myself as the sculptor and inviting their comments." This can be a safe place. My friend can vacate the premises whenever he feels invaded and at risk. Performers have no such refuge once they are before the audience. The decision to be a performer is a signal to the world and to oneself that one is open, vulnerable, available, and willing to share one's vision of reality with any who will hear.

The nature of the risk-taking of the performer is a magnified image of the personal plunge we make into the deepest places within ourselves. As we reveal our inner world to others, our reality is enhanced, emboldened, made larger than life, so to speak. This is the risk taken by the great performers every time they go before an audience. It is the essence of the quality of a star: elusive, ineffable, rarely seen, but immediately and universally recognized.

This element of risk-taking may herald the opening of the listener to the performer: the ears perk up, the heart opens and begins receiving something from the heart of the musician. There is a humanness about our willingness to open to one another, a quality that connects and binds us in immutable ways. The vulnerability of another touches that chord of tenderness within and we are moved to respond. Music is the connector, the mythic artery. The musician provides us with a human counterpart of ourselves to whom we can relate. To be one with the music is uplifting; to be one with the musician is divine.

The exchange between musicians and listeners

154

always requires certain ingredients: openness; contact with one's own and the other's center; willingness to reach out and risk; a kind of self-forgetting; compassion. The ingredients remain the same, but each encounter is new and different from every other. It is always a fresh moment, a new space (even in the same room the space is shaped differently every time), and evokes new attitudes and emotions, new physical and spiritual states in the participants. A new ritual is taking place, an unprecedented journey down a pristine path with beings who are freshly born into this moment. This is the element that makes live performance so exciting, so dynamic and joyful. Through the ancient form of musical performance, something new emerges, something of this moment that has never happened but will always be happening—an archetypal encounter.

Before the conversation begins, the musician tunes herself to the listeners. Through opening her heart, she contacts the heart of those with whom she will communicate. As this contact is made (perhaps as the musician tunes her instrument), the nature of the encounter begins to unfold. If contact seems tenuous before the music begins, it may help to play some sort of invocation, a calling of the spirit to be present during the performance. It may be easier to establish contact if the program has not been decided upon in advance. As much as the performer may feel she knows about her audience, she will find that meeting them each time as if for the first time and acknowledging their newness, this now-ness, necessitates a flexible program, open to change at any time.

The performer begins by inviting the listener into her world; the listener has the choice of entering or remaining outside that world, perhaps in the middle ground of the music. His response depends upon his own willingness to be open and vulnerable, to take the risk of exposing his own inner reality to the performer. This happens nonverbally, perhaps with no outward sign of response. The opening is silent, like that of a flower unfolding to the rays of the sun, drinking it in, exuding the fragrance of its essence, enhancing and reflecting the life around it. When the listener responds in this way, the performer feels it and is fed by the response. Thus the two-way communication begins.

Trusting in this process, the musician plays to the listener, relating the contents of her inner reality: hope, terror, gladness, despair, darkness, tenderness, fear, joy. The heart of the musician spills out its contents through her music and enters the heart of the listener. Ego, personality, appearance—none of these separating devices can block this flow from one heart to another. The music is unobstructable. The space is shaped, expanded, transformed by the sound. Boundaries fade and dissolve. The sound flows in, around, through the musician, the instrument, the space, the listener. Past and future disappear, and only this moment's reality is available for transmission. The listener, moved by the message, responds with his own fear, desire, pain, joy, sent out in silence and carried by the music back to the musician. A conversation ensues, wordless and heartfelt, between two beings, two spirits.

As the musician receives the response of the listener, she is moved, changed, inspired in ways that influence and expand the music she plays. Those sounds which began as a statement about herself become an answer, a response to the heart of the listener. Through this interchange, healing occurs. We are made whole by the recognition and acceptance of our inner selves; through music the performer and the listener are both healed. The equality of the relationship cannot be questioned except by that separating aspect of ourselves, the ego. The spirit knows we are one and thus identical in our need for healing. When the performer realizes this and works with it, she brings herself and her listeners into wholeness, holiness.

Even after the music ends, the vibrations that carried healing seem to continue shaping the space, moving into the unified field where all sound and all music reside. That field is thus enriched and enlivened by the sacred music entering it. The healing interchange between performer and listener affects this field and all of nature: the planet, consciousness, God.

Exercise: The Message of the Heart

This exercise requires a partner, preferably someone with whom you feel close. If you both have instruments, have them at hand.

Sit together quietly for a few moments, eyes closed, breathing gently. As your breath flows in and out, think of something you would like to communicate to your friend: a feeling, an image, some part of your inner reality. As your partner continues sitting quietly, let wordless sounds emerge from you, or begin playing your instrument. Imagine the soundless sound or the music as an artery, carrying a stream of images from your heart to the heart of your partner. Let the sounds continue until you feel a silent response coming from your friend back to you, carried on the

157

sounds you are making. In the shared silence
that follows, feel how your heart has opened and expanded through the communication.

Reverse roles and repeat the exercise.

The Sacred Connection

Just as the music we play continues pulsing outward in the field long after the sound has faded from our audial awareness, so the consequences of divine communication through music also live on, unseen and immeasurable. When two hearts have opened to each other, they never again close completely. Once an opening has appeared, the heart can continue to expand until it is spacious enough to hold the pain and love of the whole world. The conversation that began between the performer and the listener persists in different forms far beyond the performance itself. The musician moves on to other music, other audiences, changed and enlivened by the encounter of that moment. The listener goes back to the ordinary, mundane world, seemingly the same person but not altogether the same. The music continues as inaudible vibration, moving through unified fields to join and become one with the primal sound of the cosmos.

The musician may often be aware of the sacred nature of performance; the listener is less likely to understand his vital role as recipient of the music and as giver of his own inner music. He may not feel the full measure of his gift or realize that he has given far more than the price of admission and some applause. He may leave without knowing that he is an equal partner in the performance and in the healing process that has taken place.

Patients rely on healers to make them well. If they understand that healers, too, are in search of wholeness, that patients are also called upon to heal the ones who have come to their aid, the healing process is complete and perfect for both. In the same way, if the listener knows that both he and the performer are needed to heal, then a sacred healing ritual can result. The strength of the healing, its validity and permanence, is in direct proportion to the degree of conscious engagement of the listener and the musician in the process.

The listener usually needs to be educated concerning this process. He may have little knowledge of his sense of responsibility for the performance. To be entertained—that is the legacy of the electronic age, to be handed all and to give nothing of ourselves in return. With the New-Age consciousness of the personal and global transformation now unfolding, there can be no such passivity. We are one, and since we are growing in awareness of that oneness, we can no longer remain uninvolved.

The listener whose heart has opened to the performer can open to life and all its forms: pain, sorrow, happiness, suffering, growth, creativity. Once we begin experiencing life with open-heartedness, its exquisite beauty combines with its terror and awe to reveal what we've been missing, which we no longer choose to avoid or deny. Pain may dissolve in the wonder of the love our hearts contain; fearlessly we might begin to connect with others in spacious, loving ways, just as the music and the performer have connected with us as listeners.

This may not happen in a single performance. However, the miracle of love is an instantaneous phenomenon, present in every moment. Once we have felt it, we are never again the same. Once we have even briefly experienced true communion, connection, and oneness with another, our old ideas about separateness begin to give way.

Heart experience and spiritual communication transform us from separate, unconnected individuals to expressions of wholeness, one with the ground of being. The sacred connection made through a conscious, healing encounter between musician and listener holds the potential of transformative power. It is available to every musician who performs and to every person who listens. The choice to connect with that power, to transform ourselves and the world through the life and beauty of music, is ours to make.

So Much More . . .

Two friends of mine who are musicians wrote a wonderful song which begins: "We are so much more than this." As the final pages of this book are being written, the phrase "so much more" repeats and repeats in my head and heart.

Music is total, complete, yet utterly unbounded and infinite. Any attempt to capture its inherent wholeness in words is ultimately futile. As creators and listeners and performers of music, we are also whole and yet changing, growing, unlimited. Discovering our wholeness, our holiness, is as difficult and everlasting a search as trying to bring music into a definable, contained space.

There can be no conclusion to our quest, just as there are no endings in life or in sound. We can only continue being, allowing, feeling, thinking, experiencing life and music as illimitable, unbounded, eternal. Those things left out will eventually be found in our music and in ourselves. Essentially, life is orderly, perfect, clear, and beautiful. It is also unpredictable, filled with terror and change and enormous energy.

Let us honor that life with fearlessness and surrender; it is the only dance for now. Let the music play, let the dance go on. There is so much more. . . .

Bibliography

Arguelles, Jose and Miriam. *The Feminine Spacious as the Sky*. Boulder, Colorado: Shambhala, 1977.
——. *Mandala*. Boulder, Colorado: Shambhala, 1972.
——, Jose. *The Transformative Vision*. Boulder, Colorado: Shambhala, 1975.
Berger, John. *About Looking*. New York: Pantheon, 1980.
——. *Ways of Seeing*. New York: Penguin, 1977.
Brooks, Charles. *Sensory Awareness*. Santa Barbara, California: Ross-Erikson, 1974.
Campbell, Joseph. *The Masks of God: Oriental Mythology*. New York: Penguin, 1976.
Charon, Jean E. *The Unknown Spirit*. London: Coventure Ltd., 1983.
Chase, Mildred Portney. *Just Being at the Piano*. Culver City, California: Peace Press, 1981.
Course in Miracles, A. Farmingdale, New York: Coleman Graphics, 1975.
Eliade, Mircea. *Myth and Reality*. New York: Harper and Row, 1963.
Ferguson, Marilyn. *The Aquarian Conspiracy*. Los Angeles: J. P. Tarcher, 1983.
Field, Joanna. *On Not Being Able to Paint*. Los Angeles: J. P. Tarcher, 1983.
Hamel, Peter Michael. *Through Music to the Self*. Boulder, Colorado: Shambhala, 1979.

Harwood, A. C. *The Way of a Child.* London: Rudolf Steiner Press, 1979.

Hayward, Jeremy. *Perceiving Ordinary Magic.* Boulder, Colorado: Shambhala, 1984.

Highwater, Jamake. *The Primal Mind.* New York: Meridian, 1982.

Houston, Jean. *The Possible Human.* Los Angeles: J. P. Tarcher, 1982.

Iglehart, Hallie. *Woman Spirit.* San Francisco, California: Harper and Row, 1983.

Joy, Brugh. *Joy's Way.* Los Angeles: J. P. Tarcher, 1979.

Kandinsky, Wassily. *Concerning the Spiritual in Art.* New York: Dover, 1977.

Kenny, Carolyn. *The Mythic Artery.* Atascadero, California: Ridgeview, 1982.

Keyes, Laurel. *Toning.* Santa Monica, California: DeVorss, 1973.

Khan, Hazrat Inayat. *The Music of Life.* Santa Fe, New Mexico: Omega Press, 1983.

——. *The Mysticism of Sound.* Geneva, Switzerland: International Headquarters Sufi Movement, 1979.

Krieger, Dolores. *The Therapeutic Touch.* Englewood Cliffs, New Jersey: Prentice-Hall, 1979.

Leonard, George. *The Silent Pulse.* New York: E. P. Dutton, 1978.

——. *The Transformation.* New York: Delacorte, 1972.

Levine, Stephen. *Meetings at the Edge.* Garden City, New York: Doubleday, 1984.

——. *Who Dies?* Garden City, New York: Doubleday, 1982.

Lingerman, Hal A. *The Healing Energies of Music.* Wheaton, Illinois: Theosophical Publishing House, 1983.

Lowen, Alexander. *Pleasure.* New York: Penguin, 1975.

Maritain, Jacques. *Creative Intuition in Art and Poetry.* Princeton, New Jersey: Princeton University Press, 1977.

Memmler, Ruth Lundeen and Dena Lin Wood. *The Human Body in Health and Disease.* Philadelphia: J. B. Lippincott, 1977.

Moss, Richard. *The I That Is We.* Millbrae, California: Celestial Arts, 1981.

Neumann, Erich. *Art and the Creative Unconscious*. Princeton, New Jersey: Princeton University Press, 1974.

Nilsson, Lennart. *Behold Man*. Boston: Little, Brown and Company, 1973.

Noe, Jae Jah. *Do You See What I See?* Wheaton, Illinois: Theosophical Publishing House, 1977.

Prather, Hugh. *A Book of Games*. Garden City, New York: Doubleday, 1981.

————. *The Quiet Answer*. Garden City, New York: Doubleday, 1982.

————. *There is a Place Where You Are Not Alone*. Garden City, New York: Doubleday, 1980.

Progoff, Ira. *The Practice of Process Meditation*. New York: Dialogue House Library, 1980.

Ram Dass. *Grist for the Mill*. New York: Bantam, 1979.

Reck, David. *Music of the Whole Earth*. New York: Charles Scribners and Sons, 1977.

Richards, M. C. *Centering*. Middletown, Connecticut: Wesleyan University Press, 1964.

————. *The Crossing Point*. Middletown, Connecticut. Wesleyan University Press, 1973.

————. *Toward Wholeness: Rudolf Steiner Education in America*. Middletown, Connecticut: Wesleyan University Press, 1980.

Ristad, Eloise. *A Soprano On Her Head*. Moab, Utah: Real People Press, 1982.

Rudhyar, Dane. *Crisis, Culture, and Creativity*. Wheaton, Illinois: Theosophical Publishing House, 1977.

————. *The Rebirth of Hindu Music*. New York: Samuel Weiser, 1979.

Shankar, Ravi. *My Music, My Life*. New York: Simon and Schuster, 1968.

Sheldrake, Rupert. *A New Science of Life*. Los Angeles: J. P. Tarcher, 1981.

Steiner, Rudolf. *The Inner Nature of Music and the Experience of Tone*. Spring Valley, New York: The Anthroposophic Press, 1983.

Taylor, Jeremy. *Dreamwork*. New York: Paulist Press, 1983.

Trungpa, Chogyam. *Shambhala, The Sacred Path of the*

165

Warrior. Boulder, Colorado: Shambhala, 1984.

Whiteside, Abby. *Mastering the Chopin Etudes.* New York: Charles Scribner's Sons, 1969.

Wilbur, Ken. *No Boundary.* Boulder, Colorado: Shambhala, 1981.

Zuckerkandl, Victor. *Man the Musician.* Princeton, New Jersey: Princeton University Press, 1973.

———. *Sound and Symbol.* Princeton, New Jersey: Princeton University Press, 1969.

We have another Quest book on music called—

The Healing Energies of Music *By Hal Lingerman*
Good music can help restore good health—physical, emotional, or mental. It can be an aid to meditation. It can increase our mental power—enhance our devotion to life. Here are hundreds of selections from Bach to Beethoven to Johnny Cash, each with a distinct healing power of its own.

Quest also publishes books on reincarnation, astrology, mysticism, transpersonal psychology, and comparative religion.

Quest Books
306 West Geneva Road
Wheaton, Illinois 60187